P · O · C · K · E · T · S

BUILDINGS

CHRYSLER
BUILDING,
NEW YORK

WAT SORASAK,
SUKHOTHAI,
THAILAND

CRUCK-FRAMED
HOUSE

P · O · C · K · E · T · S

BUILDINGS

Written by
PHILIP WILKINSON

ST. GEORGE
IN THE EAST,
LONDON

STONE
WINDMILL

DORLING KINDERSLEY
London • New York • Stuttgart

A DK PUBLISHING BOOK

www.dk.com

Editors	Suzanne Melia,
	Neil Bridges
Art editor	Heather Blackham
Senior editor	Susan McKeever
Senior art editor	Helen Senior
Picture research	Caroline Brooke
Production	Louise Barratt
Consultant	Cany Ash
US editor	Jill Hamilton

First American Edition, 1995
4 6 8 10 9 7 5 3
Published in the United States by
Dorling Kindersley Publishing, Inc.,
95 Madison Avenue, New York, New York 10016
Copyright © 1995 Dorling Kindersley Ltd., London

Library of Congress Cataloging-in Publication Data
Wilkinson, Phil
    Buildings / written by Philip Wilkinson. – 1st American ed.
    p. cm. – (A Dorling Kindersley pocket)
    Includes index.
    ISBN 1–56458–885–8
    1. Architecture–Juvenile literature. [1. Architecture.]
I. Title. II. Series.
NA2555.W483 1995
720–dc20   94–24705
                                                    CIP
                                                      AC

Color reproduction by Colourscan, Singapore
Printed and bound in Italy by L.E.G.O.

CONTENTS

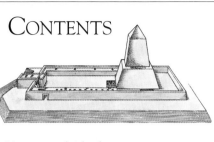

How to use this book 8

HOW TO USE THIS BOOK

These pages show you how to use Pockets: Buildings.
The book is divided into several historical sections,
covering the most important architectural styles
and building techniques of that period. There is
an introductory section at the front, and a reference
section at the back.

HISTORICAL PERIODS
The buildings in this book are
arranged according to the time
they were built. In each historical
section, you will find information
on the most important styles of
architecture and examples of
outstanding buildings of the time.

Feature box

Corner coding

Heading

Introduction

Label

THE EUROPEAN RENAISSANCE

FRENCH RENAISSANCE
THE RENAISSANCE CAME later to France than it did to
Italy. The first French Renaissance buildings were
designed in the 16th century, and often show a
combination of Gothic and classical details. Square-
headed windows, steeply sloping roofs, and a restrained
use of ornament are the
trademarks of the style.

Caption

CORNER CODING
Corners of the pages
are color coded to
remind you which
historical section
you are in.

☐ EARLY
CIVILIZATIONS

☐ MEDIEVAL
BUILDINGS

☐ THE EUROPEAN
RENAISSANCE

☐ THE
INDUSTRIAL AGE

☐ MODERN
ARCHITECTURE

HEADING
This describes the
subject of the page.
This page is about the
French Renaissance.
If a subject continues
over several pages, the
same heading applies.

INTRODUCTION
This provides a clear,
general overview of the
subject. After reading
this, you should have
an idea what the pages
are about.

CAPTIONS AND
ANNOTATIONS
Each illustration has a
caption. Annotations, in
italics, point out features
of an illustration and
usually have leader lines.

RUNNING HEADS
These remind you which section you are in. The left-hand page gives the section name. The right-hand page gives the subject. This page on the French Renaissance is in The European Renaissance section.

FACT BOXES
Many pages have a fact box. These contain at-a-glance information about the subject. This fact box gives details, such as how many people once lived in the Palace of Versailles.

Running head   *Annotation*   *Fact box*

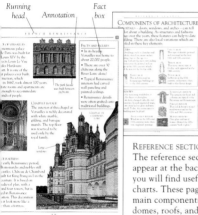

REFERENCE SECTION
The reference section pages are yellow and appear at the back of the book. On these, you will find useful facts, figures, and charts. These pages describe some of the main components of architecture, such as domes, roofs, and arches, and contain a list of famous architects and their buildings.

LABELS
For extra clarity, some pictures have labels. They may provide extra information, or identify a picture when it is not obvious from the text. A label helps to locate each building.

INDEX
At the back of the book, an easy-to-use index lists the main subjects, buildings, and architects in alphabetical order. The index is a fast, direct route to a specific person, building, or style of architecture.

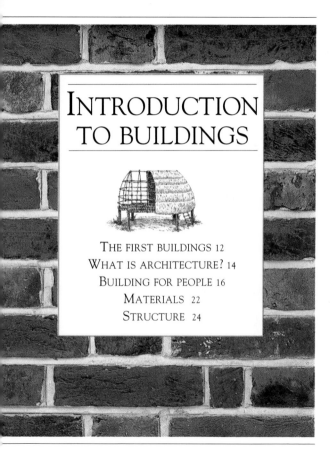

INTRODUCTION
TO BUILDINGS

THE FIRST BUILDINGS

PEOPLE HAVE ALWAYS NEEDED shelter from the elements, and very early in human history our ancestors began to construct buildings to live in. They used whatever materials were to hand, such as wood, earth, stone, and animal skins. Basic structures soon evolved with wooden frames, or solid walls of mud or stone.

BRUSHWOOD HUT
About 380,000 years ago, our ancestors created simple shelters out of closely packed brushwood held in place by rocks. Huts like these were only occupied for part of the year. People moved about often to search for food.

Rocks held the structure in place.

These huts in Chile are the earliest known dwellings in the Americas.

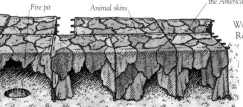

Fire pit   *Animal skins*

WOODEN DWELLINGS
Rows of wooden-framed huts were built in Monte Verde, Chile, in c.12,000 B.C. The frames were covered in animal skins, and pits were sunk into the floors for fires.

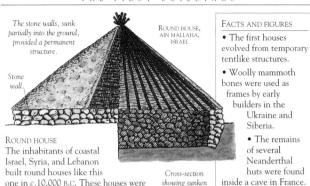

The stone walls, sunk partially into the ground, provided a permanent structure.

ROUND HOUSE, AIN MALLAHA, ISRAEL

Stone wall

Cross-section showing sunken interior.

FACTS AND FIGURES

• The first houses evolved from temporary tentlike structures.

• Woolly mammoth bones were used as frames by early builders in the Ukraine and Siberia.

• The remains of several Neanderthal huts were found inside a cave in France.

ROUND HOUSE

The inhabitants of coastal Israel, Syria, and Lebanon built round houses like this one in c.10,000 B.C. These houses were built by people who stayed in one place gathering wild food.

THE FIRST TOWNS

By c.6000 B.C., early towns, like Çatal Hüyük in Turkey, were being built. Their mud-brick houses nestled close together. Access was through trapdoors in the flat roofs, which could be used as work areas when it was not too hot.

SETTLEMENT, ÇATAL HÜYÜK, TURKEY

Ladders lead from the roofs down into the buildings.

Flat roof

Yard

13

WHAT IS ARCHITECTURE?

THE FIRST SIMPLE SHELTERS and houses were built by
the people who lived in them. But for larger or more
complex structures, such as temples, public buildings,
and royal palaces, the process must be planned. These
buildings are designed by an
architect to be functional,
attractive, and comfortable. The
site is prepared, the materials
ordered, and a workforce
organized. Architects often have
their own distinctive style.

STONEMASON
Some of the most
important workers on a
Roman building site were
the masons. Later, during
the medieval period, the
master mason played the
role of architect.

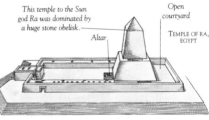

*This temple to the Sun
god Ra was dominated by
a huge stone obelisk.*

Altar

*Open
courtyard*

TEMPLE OF RA,
EGYPT

Causeway

*Second
temple*

EGYPTIAN TEMPLE
One of the first architects we know is Imhotep, designer
of the first pyramid. The Egyptians produced some of the
biggest buildings of the ancient world. Building temples,
like this one at Abu Ghurab, involved transporting huge
amounts of stone by a large workforce.

SUNDIAL, REIMS CATHEDRAL
Buildings usually do more than just provide shelter. Even the humblest house will have some decoration that reflects the taste of its builder or owner. The sundial on this French cathedral is a functional piece of decoration that also tells worshipers when it is time for Mass.

GARGOYLES
The gargoyles on Gothic cathedrals are guardians against evil spirits, and are often carved in a style quite at odds with the rest of the building.

Some gargoyles cover water spouts.

ART GALLERY
Architects often become as famous as their buildings. This art museum was designed by Frank Lloyd Wright. Visitors take an elevator to the top, then walk down a long spiral ramp to view the pictures. The distinctive form of the ramp is visible from the outside.

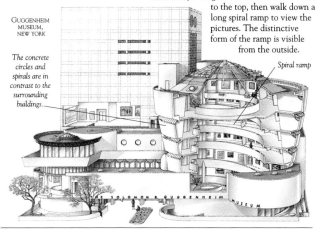

GUGGENHEIM MUSEUM, NEW YORK

The concrete circles and spirals are in contrast to the surrounding buildings.

Spiral ramp

SOLOMON R. GUGGENHEIM MUSEUM

BUILDING FOR PEOPLE

ALTHOUGH TRENDS IN architecture are often set by
large public buildings or specifically commissioned
houses, most of the buildings in the world are smaller
structures – people's homes, which sometimes also
double as their places of work. Most houses consist of
walls and a roof in various styles.

Homes and workplaces

Homes vary greatly around the world, depending on the climate
and the environment. If an area is prone to flooding, for
example, houses may be built on stilts; in a desert, thick walls
will keep a house cool
during the day, but
warm at night.

Thatch

Timber frame

Stilt

STILT HOUSE,
THAILAND

FACTS AND FIGURES

• Longhouses can be
150 ft (45 m) in length.

• In the hot Australian
desert, some houses
have been built
underground.

• Elegant town
houses, built in towns
in the 18th century,
housed the wealthy.

• The Industrial
Age saw many more
houses being put up by
professional builders.

STILT HOUSE
Raised on poles to keep it away from the floods of the
rainy season, this Thai house is made of wood and
thatch. Houses like this have been built in
southeastern Asia for hundreds of years.

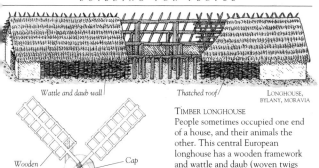

Wattle and daub wall

Thatched roof

LONGHOUSE,
BYLANY, MORAVIA

Wooden sails

Cap

STONE
WINDMILL

TIMBER LONGHOUSE
People sometimes occupied one end of a house, and their animals the other. This central European longhouse has a wooden framework and wattle and daub (woven twigs plastered with clay) walls.

WINDMILL
Some buildings are designed for a very specialized function. The sails of a windmill are mounted on a cap which can be turned into the wind.

GREAT CUMBERLAND
PLACE, LONDON,
ENGLAND

WESTERN TOWN HOUSE
In the limited space of cities, more room can be made by building high. In this way the requirements of the rich, including the servants' rooms in the attic and the kitchens in the basement, could be fitted into a tall, elegant house. This town house in London was built in 1790.

Public buildings

Temples, churches, assembly halls, and places of government are often some of the most interesting buildings. Designed to be used by large groups of people, they can be large and complex, sometimes with many rooms arranged around a large central hall. Public buildings are often adorned with decoration that reflects their use – a senate house, for example, may have statues representing justice or democracy.

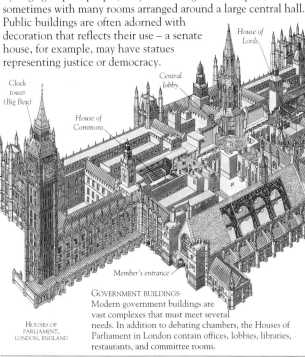

House of Lords

Central lobby

Clock tower (Big Ben)

House of Commons

Member's entrance

HOUSES OF PARLIAMENT, LONDON, ENGLAND

GOVERNMENT BUILDINGS
Modern government buildings are vast complexes that must meet several needs. In addition to debating chambers, the Houses of Parliament in London contain offices, lobbies, libraries, restaurants, and committee rooms.

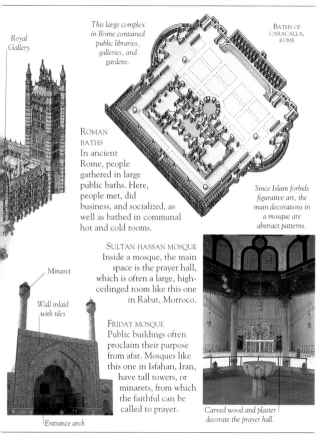

Royal Gallery

This large complex in Rome contained public libraries, galleries, and gardens.

BATHS OF CARACALLA, ROME

ROMAN BATHS
In ancient Rome, people gathered in large public baths. Here, people met, did business, and socialized, as well as bathed in communal hot and cold rooms.

Since Islam forbids figurative art, the main decorations in a mosque are abstract patterns.

SULTAN HASSAN MOSQUE
Inside a mosque, the main space is the prayer hall, which is often a large, high-ceilinged room like this one in Rabat, Morocco.

Minaret

Wall inlaid with tiles

FRIDAY MOSQUE
Public buildings often proclaim their purpose from afar. Mosques like this one in Isfahan, Iran, have tall towers, or minarets, from which the faithful can be called to prayer.

Entrance arch

Carved wood and plaster decorate the prayer hall.

Special-purpose buildings

An architect needs to think carefully about how a new building is going to be used. This is the case in the smallest, most straightforward house, but it is even more obvious in the host of buildings designed for a more specific purpose. A railroad station, for example, will need a large trainshed and spacious areas in which passengers can move around. A concert hall will need a variety of backstage facilities, from dressing rooms to storerooms – often larger than the auditorium itself.

AIRPORT TERMINAL

Architects sometimes use form and structure to suggest the purpose of their buildings. Eero Saarinen's passenger terminal at Kennedy Airport in New York (finished in 1962) is roofed by a concrete shell that suggests a soaring bird.

Arrow slits

MEDIEVAL CASTLE

Medieval castles have thick walls for protection. Towers with arrow slits and battlements allow the defenders to fire at the enemy while remaining hidden.

Concrete roof

TWA TERMINAL, NEW YORK

Roof support

Large windows

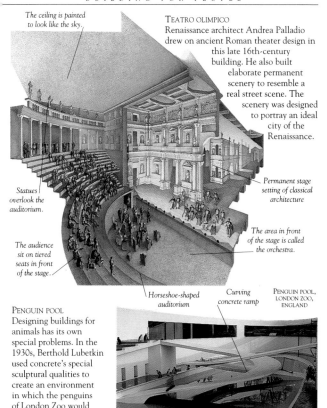

The ceiling is painted to look like the sky.

TEATRO OLIMPICO
Renaissance architect Andrea Palladio drew on ancient Roman theater design in this late 16th-century building. He also built elaborate permanent scenery to resemble a real street scene. The scenery was designed to portray an ideal city of the Renaissance.

Permanent stage setting of classical architecture

Statues overlook the auditorium.

The area in front of the stage is called the orchestra.

The audience sit on tiered seats in front of the stage.

Horseshoe-shaped auditorium

Curving concrete ramp

PENGUIN POOL, LONDON ZOO, ENGLAND

PENGUIN POOL
Designing buildings for animals has its own special problems. In the 1930s, Berthold Lubetkin used concrete's special sculptural qualities to create an environment in which the penguins of London Zoo would feel at home.

MATERIALS

THE EARLIEST BUILDINGS were
made of naturally occurring
materials, such as wood,
stone, and grass. But, about
6,000 years ago, people
learned to bake clay
bricks. Today, buildings
combine natural and
manufactured materials.

WOOD
Lumber is widely used for roof
frameworks, floors, and window
frames. Trees are specially planted
to supply lumber for building.

Thatched roof

Lath

Rafter

Hazel rod

Layer of thatch

Modern slate

GRASS
Straw from grasses
or reeds is one of the
oldest roofing materials. It is
used for lightweight roofing in
Africa, and thick waterproof
coverings in Europe.

SLATES
A common roofing
material, slate is a stone
that can be split into
thin sheets, then nailed
onto wooden rafters.

Granite

STONE
From hard, durable granite to the softer limestones that can be cut and carved, stone is one of the oldest and most resilient of the building materials.

BRICK
Earth pressed into molds and baked in the sun or in a kiln produces bricks. Simple to lay, and very long-lasting, bricks have been used for thousands of years.

Modern engineering brick

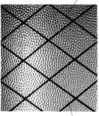

Glass

Lead frame

GLASS
For centuries, glass was an expensive luxury that could only be made in small pieces. Medieval stained-glass makers used these small pieces in their designs. It was only in the 19th century that glass could be produced in large sheets.

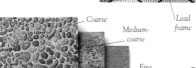

Coarse

Medium-coarse

Fine texture

CONCRETE
The Romans invented concrete and used it extensively. This mixture of sand, gravel, and cement was not used again until the 18th century.

METAL
The Industrial Revolution of the 18th and 19th centuries saw an increase in the use of metal in buildings. Iron pillars and steel frameworks held up buildings from warehouses to office blocks.

The use of iron and steel enabled the construction of multistory buildings.

STRUCTURE

WHATEVER MATERIALS are used, whether natural or manufactured, buildings have two basic types of structure. They can either be frame buildings, with a sturdy, skeleton-like frame holding up the roof, or solid buildings, with heavy walls taking the weight of the entire structure.

FRAME BUILDING
Wood-framed buildings were common in 16th-century Europe.

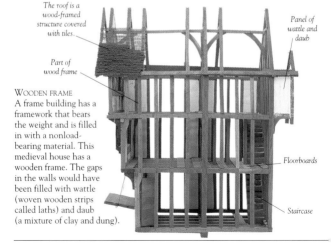

The roof is a wood-framed structure covered with tiles.

Part of wood frame

Panel of wattle and daub

WOODEN FRAME
A frame building has a framework that bears the weight and is filled in with a nonload-bearing material. This medieval house has a wooden frame. The gaps in the walls would have been filled with wattle (woven wooden strips called laths) and daub (a mixture of clay and dung).

Floorboards

Staircase

SOLID WALL AND FRAME ROOF

Many small buildings have solid walls and a frame roof. This corner of a small house shows a solid wall of bricks, and a roof consisting of a wooden framework covered in plain tiles.

Frame roof is light and easy to build.

ROOF TYPES

The simplest roof designs are the hipped and pavilion, with sloping ends. More complex layouts, like the gable-and-valley or sloped turret, are used on ornate buildings.

GABLE-AND-VALLEY

PAVILION

SLOPED TURRET

HIPPED

SOLID BUILDING

In a solid building, the entire wall bears the weight of the structure. The Pantheon in Rome, Italy, is a solid building with walls of brick-faced concrete and a solid domed roof. A system of buttresses (supports) also help hold up the building.

Concrete dome

PANTHEON, ROME

Brick-and-concrete walls

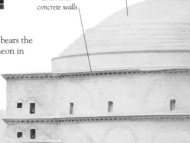

Granite columns at entrance

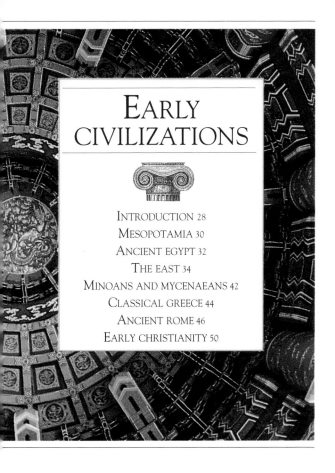

EARLY CIVILIZATIONS

INTRODUCTION

AROUND 8000 B.C., people began to live together in towns and cities. These were often ruled by powerful leaders who lived in palaces. There was usually some form of organized religion, which meant that temples had to be built. The palace and the temple were the largest buildings in early cities. Strong walls with fortified gatehouses and watchtowers defended the cities from invasion.

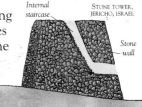

Internal staircase

STONE TOWER, JERICHO, ISRAEL

Stone wall

STONE TOWER
Jericho was one of the first cities. Building began in c.8000 B.C., and the city was surrounded with a ditch and a wall topped with this stone tower.

CLAY TABLET
The development of writing has enabled us to learn much about early people and their buildings.

TEMPLE
The cities of Mesopotamia (modern Iraq) flourished after c.4300 B.C. The niches along the walls of this temple are typical of the period c.4300-3100 B.C.

Main temple

Painted frieze

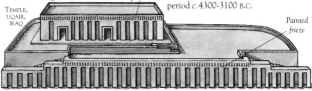

TEMPLE, UQAIR, IRAQ

STONE GATEWAY
The Hittites flourished in
Anatolia (modern Turkey)
between the 14th and
12th centuries B.C. This
stone gate remains from
the capital at Hattushash
(modern Boghazköy).

ENTRANCE GATE,
BOGHAZKÖY,
TURKEY

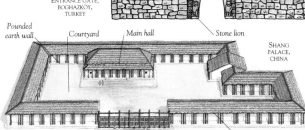

Pounded earth wall   *Courtyard*   *Main hall*   Stone lion

SHANG
PALACE,
CHINA

Timber doors   *Thatched gallery*

SHANG PALACE
The Shang civilization
reached a high point in
China in c.1600-1027 B.C.
This typical Shang palace
has a large one-room hall
with a thatched gallery.

GRECIAN VASE
Pottery provides a good
way of dating ancient
buildings. This Greek
vase is in the red-figure
style, and dates from the
period c.470-60 B.C.

VASE FROM
ANCIENT
GREECE

FACTS AND FIGURES

• Hittite houses had
clay drainpipes.

• The Egyptians
transported granite
down the River Nile.

• Kings of Babylon had
their names stamped on
individual bricks.

• The Hittites built
stone walls without
using mortar.

MESOPOTAMIA

SOME OF THE MOST IMPORTANT early civilizations developed in Iraq after c.4300 B.C. They were based around the Tigris and Euphrates Rivers, in an area known as Mesopotamia. A series of city-states evolved, some of which expanded into empires. Mud bricks molded from straw and mud were used to build everything from houses to temples.

ASSYRIAN DECORATION
The temples and palaces of the Assyrians (from the northern part of Mesopotamia) were decorated with carved stone reliefs, featuring winged figures and mythical beasts. They appeared on doorways and gates as protection.

STONE FIGURE   TERRACOTTA RELIEF

ZIGGURAT
This Sumerian temple at Ur was the first of many to be built in Mesopotamia. It dates from c.2100 B.C., and consists of a series of stepped platforms made of mud bricks. It was designed to bring the priests closer to the heavens.

The temple was dedicated to the moon god.

Niches decorated the temple walls.

ZIGGURAT AT UR

Stepped platform

ISHTAR GATE, IRAQ

Glazed bricks

- The floodplains of the rivers supplied the mud for making bricks.
- The Sumerians of southern Mesopotamia were the first people to settle in the region.
- The Assyrians, who ruled the largest empire, moved and rebuilt their capital city several times.

ISHTAR GATE
The city of Babylon dominated the region in the 6th century B.C. It was heavily fortified. This strong gatehouse is adorned with colored glazed bricks showing animal symbols of Babylonian gods on a blue background.

CITY OF KHORSABAD
Khorsabad was one of the capital cities of the Assyrians, who ruled the region from the 9th to 7th centuries B.C. The large mud-brick city contained a palace and temple complex with a tall ziggurat. The Assyrians were often involved in wars, so the city was protected from invasion by strong walls and towers.

Palace complex

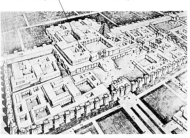

ANCIENT EGYPT

THE ANCIENT Egyptians built the first large-scale stone buildings. Many of these were tombs. Egyptian pharaohs (kings) were often buried in massive stone pyramids, which took years to construct. Egyptians also built stone temples to their gods.

PYRAMIDS
The pharaohs of the Old Kingdom (c.2815-2294 B.C.) were buried in pyramids. The Step Pyramid is the earliest. The Bent Pyramid and the Great Pyramid followed.

STEP PYRAMID   BENT PYRAMID (2723 B.C.)   GREAT PYRAMID (2528 B.C.)

Sacred inscriptions on columns

TEMPLE OF AMON-RE
The main hall contains 134 columns decorated with hieroglyphs (picture writing) and paintings of gods and kings. The central nave (aisle) of the hall is about 79 ft (24 m) high.

TEMPLE OF LUXOR

TEMPLE OF LUXOR
This statue of Ramesses II dates from 1290-1220 B.C. It is one of two identical statues that flank the entrance to the temple. The Great Colonnade, behind, rises over 65 ft (20 m).

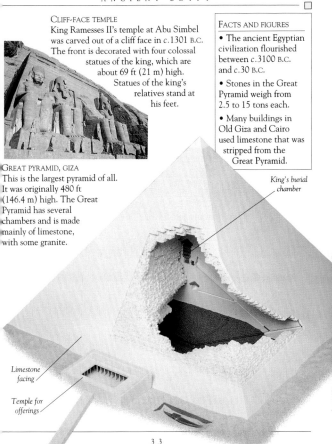

CLIFF-FACE TEMPLE

King Ramesses II's temple at Abu Simbel was carved out of a cliff face in *c.*1301 B.C. The front is decorated with four colossal statues of the king, which are about 69 ft (21 m) high. Statues of the king's relatives stand at his feet.

FACTS AND FIGURES

• The ancient Egyptian civilization flourished between *c.*3100 B.C. and *c.*30 B.C.

• Stones in the Great Pyramid weigh from 2.5 to 15 tons each.

• Many buildings in Old Giza and Cairo used limestone that was stripped from the Great Pyramid.

GREAT PYRAMID, GIZA

This is the largest pyramid of all. It was originally 480 ft (146.4 m) high. The Great Pyramid has several chambers and is made mainly of limestone, with some granite.

King's burial chamber

Limestone facing

Temple for offerings

THE EAST

DECORATED CHINESE ROOF

ANCIENT CHINESE and Japanese buildings traditionally stand on a low stone platform. Wooden columns support a heavy tiled roof. The space between the supporting columns is filled with thick outer walls or light lattice screens.

WOODEN PAGODA, CHINA

Tiled roof with upturned corners

Stone base

Ancient China

Chinese architecture changed little from the Han Dynasty (206 B.C.-A.D. 220) to the 19th century. Typical Chinese buildings were wood-framed. These roofs were decorated with ornamental crests and upturned corners, and many had colored tiles.

MULTISTORY TOWER
A pagoda is a many-sided, multistory building with an odd number of floors. Each story has an ornamented overhanging roof. The first pagodas were wooden, but most that survive are of brick.

HAN DYNASTY HOUSE
A few original buildings survive from the Han Dynasty period. They are simple structures made of pounded (packed) earth, but many also featured the typical Chinese overhanging roofs. This is a pottery model of an ancient Chinese house.

INTERIOR, TEMPLE OF HEAVEN

SUPPORTING PILLARS
The largest of the three roofs of the Temple of Heaven is shown in this picture. It has 12 supporting pillars, each made from the trunk of a single tree.

TEMPLE OF HEAVEN
The Temple of Heaven in Beijing is a circular temple that dates from the 15th century. It was built for the emperor, who performed rituals of spirit worship on behalf of his people. The temple has three roofs covered with blue glazed tiles. Its interior is carved and painted, and the ceilings have coffers (sunken panels).

Gold-plated ornamental ball

The roof was the most important part of a traditional Chinese building. It was designed before the main structure of the building itself.

Each of the three circular roofs is covered with blue glazed tiles.

Load-bearing wooden framework

Brightly painted beams

Stone platform

Chinese imperial buildings

The emperors of China controlled a vast workforce and were able to build on a large scale. One grand imperial project was the Great Wall, begun by the First Emperor in about 214 B.C. Later emperors built fine capital cities. The emperors of the Ming Dynasty (1368-1644) chose Peking (now called Beijing) as their capital. It was the last and most important of the imperial cities.

The Meridian Gate was used only by the emperor.

Walls separated the imperial court from the rest of Peking.

FORBIDDEN CITY

As a capital, Peking was designed in zones. The inner area, the imperial court, was walled off from the rest of the city. The imperial court contained the emperor's quarters and buildings, such as temples, workshops, and stables. Only the imperial household and those on imperial business were allowed into the court. As a result, it was known as the "Forbidden City."

AUDIENCE HALLS

The Forbidden City is built around a series of audience halls in which the emperor received visitors. The halls are wooden buildings raised on stone platforms and supported by wooden pillars. Inside, they are brightly decorated with carved and painted woodwork. In the middle of each hall was the emperor's throne.

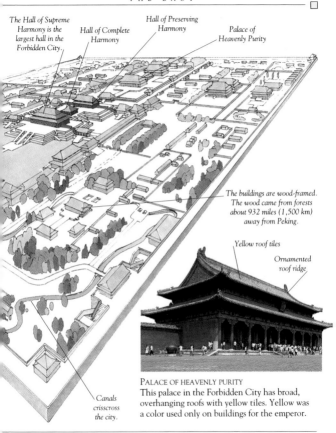

The Hall of Supreme Harmony is the largest hall in the Forbidden City.

Hall of Complete Harmony

Hall of Preserving Harmony

Palace of Heavenly Purity

The buildings are wood-framed. The wood came from forests about 932 miles (1,500 km) away from Peking.

Yellow roof tiles

Ornamented roof ridge

Canals crisscross the city.

PALACE OF HEAVENLY PURITY
This palace in the Forbidden City has broad, overhanging roofs with yellow tiles. Yellow was a color used only on buildings for the emperor.

Ancient Japan

Typical Japanese architecture developed slowly, and has changed little over the centuries. The style is influenced by climate, religion, and locally available materials, such as wood, paper, clay, and metals. Wood-framed buildings have overhanging roofs to throw off the rain and to provide shade. Structures are often raised on platforms, and walls can be opened to allow air to circulate.

The irregular design of this roof is unusual.

GOLDEN HALL
Japan's oldest Buddhist temple at Nara was built in c.A.D. 607. This is the large central hall, used for prayer and teaching. Its gently curving tiled roofs and bracketed pillars are influenced by Chinese design.

PAGODA, YAKUSHI-JI
Pagodas dominate many Japanese Buddhist sites. Their tapering height reminds Buddhists of the sacred mythical Mount Meru.

Railings with decorative carving.

Curving tiled roof

HORYU-JI TEMPLE, NARA

Bracketed pillar

ORNATE SHRINE

A close look at the corner of a shrine shows some of the common features of Japanese construction. The main framework is made of wood, with the gaps between filled with lightweight sliding screens, thin walls, and doors. Ornately carved, brightly painted wooden brackets support the overhanging tiled roof.

HEIAN JINGU SHRINE, KYOTO

Wooden brackets

TOSHOGU SHRINE

Shinto is the ancient religion of Japan, and this Shinto shrine at Nikko is over 1,000 years old. Its walls and roof show the ornate decoration painted on Japanese religious buildings. On the right is the Kara Mon Gate – a wooden gatehouse set on a massive stone base.

TOSHOGU SHRINE, NIKKO

Kara Mon Gate

FACTS AND FIGURES

- Hollowed bamboo was used to make gutters and drainpipes.

- Wooden buildings were less vulnerable to earthquakes.

- In Japanese houses, walls of translucent paper allow daylight to filter through.

- Japanese pagodas vary from three to fifteen stories, and may be as high as 120 ft (34 m).

Japanese castles

During the 16th century, local lords called daimyo became very powerful in Japan. They built strong castles as military bases and homes for themselves and their followers, warriors known as samurai. These castles had a distinctive style. They usually had a central multistory keep, or donjon, made of wood. The keep stood on a stone base and was surrounded by a network of defensive stone walls and a moat.

SAMURAI

HIMEJI CASTLE

Originally built in medieval times, Himeji is one of the finest Japanese castles. It was extended and strengthened in the early 17th century. The walls of the keep had gun loops through which defenders fired guns. Defenders could also open hidden trapdoors and throw missiles onto the enemy below.

Decorated gable

White plaster walls

Courtyard

Outer courtyard

ROOFTOPS

Fine roofs were a status symbol in Japan. The decorated gables (triangular part of a wall enclosed by a sloping roof) and roofs of Himeji Castle show that an important lord lived there.

PLAN OF HIMEJI CASTLE
The keep is surrounded by several courtyards, which are separated by stone walls and gates. An enemy would have to pass through all these courtyards to reach the keep, which was the safest place to be during a siege.

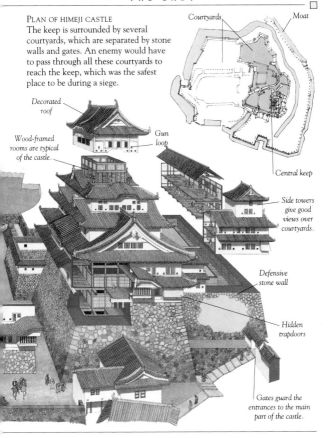

Courtyards

Moat

Courtyards

Central keep

Decorated roof

Gun loop

Wood-framed rooms are typical of the castle.

Side towers give good views over courtyards.

Defensive stone wall

Hidden trapdoors

Gates guard the entrances to the main part of the castle.

MINOANS AND MYCENAEANS

THE MINOANS LIVED on Crete, an island in the Aegean Sea. Their kings lived in large, elegant palaces, the most famous of which is the palace of Minos at Knossos. The Mycenaean culture was based around citadels (fortified cities) on the mainland of Greece. Mycenae was the home of Agamemnon, a king in Greek mythology.

CYPRESS WOOD COLUMNS
Many rooms in the palace of Minos open onto courtyards that are surrounded by columns of cypress wood.

PALACE OF MINOS
This was the largest and most complex of the Minoan palaces. It was built over a long period, and rooms seem to have been added as needed. The rooms were grouped around a central courtyard. Beautiful wall paintings called frescoes decorated many of these rooms.

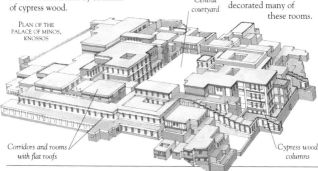

PLAN OF THE PALACE OF MINOS, KNOSSOS

Central courtyard

Corridors and rooms with flat roofs

Cypress wood columns

LION GATE

Strong stone walls surround the palace at Mycenae. The main gate of the palace is topped by a 16-ft-high(4.9 m) lintel, a horizontal cover over an opening. A relief (wall carving) showing two lions separated by a column stands on top of the lintel. The gate was built in about 1250 B.C. and is known as the "Lion Gate."

UNDERGROUND TOMB

The Treasury of Atreus dates from about 1325 B.C. This Mycenaean tomb was built by digging a circular pit, lining it with stone blocks, and then cutting the stone to make a smooth interior surface. It has one of the most impressive early domes.

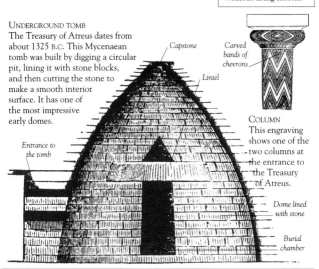

Capstone

Carved bands of chevrons

Lintel

Entrance to the tomb

COLUMN

This engraving shows one of the two columns at the entrance to the Treasury of Atreus.

Dome lined with stone

Burial chamber

CLASSICAL GREECE

THE GREEKS OF the classical period developed an elegant style of architecture with three main orders, or styles. Each order had a different design for its columns, capitals, and entablatures (the structures above the capitals). These features are best seen in the Greek temples.

CARYATID ON ERECHTHEION

CAPITALS
A Doric order column is topped with plain capitals. Ionic order capitals include decorative spiral scrolls, and capitals of the Corinthian order feature carved acanthus leaves.

DORIC   IONIC   CORINTHIAN

ERECHTHEION
The Acropolis (high city) overlooks Athens. One of its temples was the Erechtheion, which was built between 421 and 405 B.C. It is shown in its original form in this etching. Most of the columns are Ionic, although on one porch there are caryatids, columns in the shape of female figures.

FACTS AND FIGURES
• The classical period in Greece lasted from about 480 to 323 B.C.

• The three main Greek orders are Doric, Ionic, and Corinthian.

• Greek columns from the classical period appear to be straight, but are subtly curved.

• The stones that make up the Parthenon are joined together with wooden plugs.

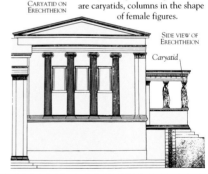

SIDE VIEW OF ERECHTHEION

Caryatid

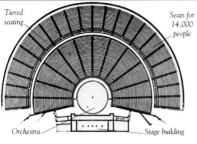

Tiered
seating

Seats for
14,000
people

Orchestra

Stage building

OPEN-AIR THEATER

The Greeks built large open-air theaters. This print shows the theatre at Epidauros, which dates from about 350 B.C. Its tiered (sloped) stone seating was arranged in a semicircle in front of the stage building. No one knows how this building looked, since only the foundations remain. The circular orchestra was a space for dancing.

PARTHENON

This temple of the Greek goddess Athena dominates the Acropolis. It is an example of the Doric order built between 447 and 432 B.C. The columns have plain capitals. They support a pediment (triangular part of wall above the entablature) that was once adorned with marble sculptures.

A band of sculpture, called a frieze, once ran behind the colonnade where it was protected.

Fluted (vertically channeled) marble columns of the Doric order

Remains of pediment

ANCIENT ROME

THE ROMANS' HUGE EMPIRE stretched from Britain to Asia and Africa. They adapted the classical style of the Greeks, adding domes, vaults, arches, and brickwork, and used concrete for the first time.

Everyday buildings

While most citizens lived in compact town houses built around courtyards, the rich also had large country houses or villas. Many of these houses were ornate and impressive. Some villas had a form of central heating called a hypocaust. Hot air from a fire flowed beneath the floors.

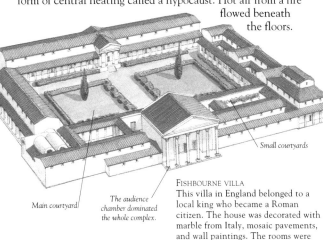

Small courtyards

Main courtyard

The audience chamber dominated the whole complex.

FISHBOURNE VILLA
This villa in England belonged to a local king who became a Roman citizen. The house was decorated with marble from Italy, mosaic pavements, and wall paintings. The rooms were arranged around a large courtyard.

TRAJAN'S MARKETS

An enormous brick block of shops and offices, these markets were built by the emperor Trajan in the early 2nd century A.D. The complex included a market hall with shops arranged in a semicircle. Everything from fabrics to spices was sold here.

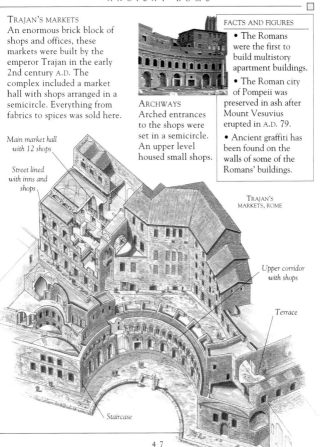

ARCHWAYS

Arched entrances to the shops were set in a semicircle. An upper level housed small shops.

FACTS AND FIGURES

• The Romans were the first to build multistory apartment buildings.

• The Roman city of Pompeii was preserved in ash after Mount Vesuvius erupted in A.D. 79.

• Ancient graffiti has been found on the walls of some of the Romans' buildings.

TRAJAN'S MARKETS, ROME

Main market hall with 12 shops

Street lined with inns and shops

Upper corridor with shops

Terrace

Staircase

Public buildings

With a large empire, the Romans had the labor force and resources to construct huge public buildings. These included temples, markets, basilicas (where courts were held and business conducted), and places of entertainment. Such large buildings showed the power and status of the emperors.

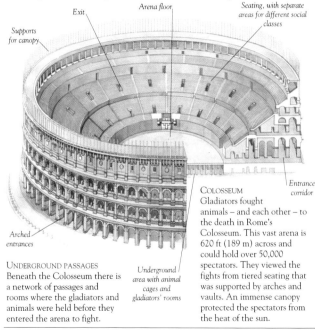

Exit

Arena floor

Seating, with separate areas for different social classes

Supports for canopy

Arched entrances

Entrance corridor

Underground area with animal cages and gladiators' rooms

UNDERGROUND PASSAGES
Beneath the Colosseum there is a network of passages and rooms where the gladiators and animals were held before they entered the arena to fight.

COLOSSEUM
Gladiators fought animals – and each other – to the death in Rome's Colosseum. This vast arena is 620 ft (189 m) across and could hold over 50,000 spectators. They viewed the fights from tiered seating that was supported by arches and vaults. An immense canopy protected the spectators from the heat of the sun.

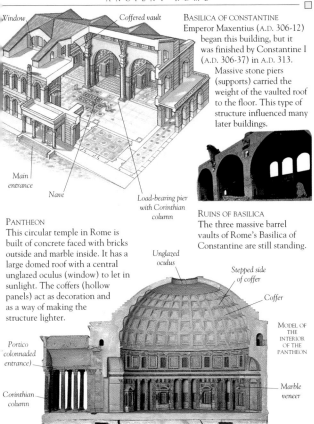

Window

Coffered vault

Main entrance

Nave

Load-bearing pier with Corinthian column

BASILICA OF CONSTANTINE
Emperor Maxentius (A.D. 306-12) began this building, but it was finished by Constantine I (A.D. 306-37) in A.D. 313. Massive stone piers (supports) carried the weight of the vaulted roof to the floor. This type of structure influenced many later buildings.

RUINS OF BASILICA
The three massive barrel vaults of Rome's Basilica of Constantine are still standing.

PANTHEON
This circular temple in Rome is built of concrete faced with bricks outside and marble inside. It has a large domed roof with a central unglazed oculus (window) to let in sunlight. The coffers (hollow panels) act as decoration and as a way of making the structure lighter.

Unglazed oculus

Stepped side of coffer

Coffer

MODEL OF THE INTERIOR OF THE PANTHEON

Portico colonnaded entrance)

Corinthian column

Marble veneer

EARLY CHRISTIANITY

CONSTANTINE was the first Roman emperor to adopt Christianity in the 4th century. Early Christians adapted the Roman aisled basilica for their first churches. The resulting style of architecture became common in the eastern or Byzantine Empire, and is often known as the Byzantine style.

BYZANTINE CAPITALS
The Byzantines evolved their own style of decoration. Some Byzantine capitals are like the Greek Corinthian type. Others have openwork or finely carved basketwork designs.

CUBICAL   COMPOSITE   CORINTHIAN

FACTS AND FIGURES

• Many Byzantine churches are decorated with beautiful mosaics.

• The dome of Hagia Sophia measures 107 ft (32.6 m) across.

• Riots in A.D. 532 led to the destruction of many buildings in Constantinople.

• Byzantine cities had defensive walls up to 40 ft (12 m) high.

SANTA SABINA FACADE

High windows

SANTA SABINA INTERIOR

SANTA SABINA
This basilica-type church was built on the Aventine hill in Rome in the 5th century. Its nave is flanked by arches with Corinthian columns. A curved sanctuary houses the high altar.

Curved sanctuary

HAGIA SOPHIA

The church of Hagia Sophia (the Divine Wisdom) was built in Constantinople (modern Istanbul) during the 6th century. It is supported by massive piers and flanked by two semidomes.

Dome took six years to build.

Minaret

THE GREAT DOME

Inside the great church, the dome, pierced by 40 windows, seems to float above the vast central space, creating a church quite unlike the basilica design.

MINARETS

The dome of Hagia Sophia makes an imposing silhouette. The minarets were added later, when the Muslims conquered the city and turned this church into a mosque.

HAGIA SOPHIA, ISTANBUL

MEDIEVAL BUILDINGS

INTRODUCTION

MANY BUILDINGS OF the medieval age were linked with the rise of organized religion. In the Far East, Hinduism and Buddhism were well established, while Islam was spreading in the Middle East, North Africa, and Spain. In western Europe, great Gothic cathedrals demonstrated the faith of the people and the great power of the Church.

WAT SORASAK, SUKHOTHAI, THAILAND

Elephant sculptures surround the base of the stupa.

REIMS CATHEDRAL, FRANCE

BUDDHIST STUPA
Buddhism spread throughout India, Southeast Asia, China, and Japan. The typical Buddhist building was the stupa, an earth mound clad in brick or stone. It was often decorated with sacred animal carvings.

CHRISTIAN CATHEDRAL
Christians built Gothic-style cathedrals all over Western Europe. Armies of laborers, with specialized workers such as stonemasons, glassmakers, and carpenters, often took decades to build them.

Minaret

AL AZHAR MOSQUE,
CAIRO, EGYPT

Dome

FACTS AND FIGURES

• In Burma alone there are the remains of 5,000 Buddhist stupas.

• The Khmers of Cambodia built the largest temples.

• Christians built huge monasteries that often included hospitals.

• A mosque at Marrakech in Morocco, Africa, has a minaret over 200 ft (60 m) high.

ISLAMIC MOSQUE
As the Muslims conquered new peoples, Islamic builders took the traditional mosque design farther afield. There was usually a domed prayer hall, a courtyard, and at least one minaret.

AZTEC CALENDAR STONE
The Aztecs were skilled builders and scientists. They represented their calendar on stones like the one above.

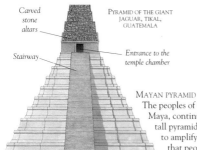

Carved stone altars

PYRAMID OF THE GIANT JAGUAR, TIKAL, GUATEMALA

Stairway

Entrance to the temple chamber

MAYAN PYRAMID
The peoples of Central America, such as the Maya, continued to build temples on top of tall pyramids. Many temples were shaped to amplify the voices of the priests, so that people at ground level could follow the ceremonies.

MEDIEVAL VERNACULAR

IN MEDIEVAL EUROPE, everyday buildings were built with whatever materials were available. Builders used a simple style that was influenced by the local materials and climate rather than the latest architectural fashion. As a result, these structures – known as vernacular buildings – were built in the same style for hundreds of years.

Cruck frame

WATTLE AND DAUB
Many walls in this period were made of wattle (wooden strips) and daub (a mixture of clay and dung).

CRUCK-FRAMED HOUSE
An early type of frame building was the cruck frame. The main beams made an upside-down V-shape, visible at both ends of the building. The space between was filled with wattle and daub.

SECTION OF LONDON BRIDGE, ENGLAND

Stone chapel of St. Thomas

Wooden frame

Iron railing

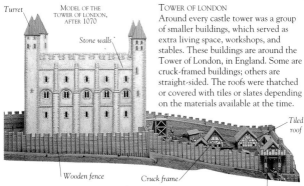

Turret

MODEL OF THE
TOWER OF LONDON,
AFTER 1070

Stone walls

TOWER OF LONDON
Around every castle tower was a group of smaller buildings, which served as extra living space, workshops, and stables. These buildings are around the Tower of London, in England. Some are cruck-framed buildings; others are straight-sided. The roofs were thatched or covered with tiles or slates depending on the materials available at the time.

Tiled roof

Wooden fence

Cruck frame

Straight-sided buildings were popular in the later medieval period.

LONDON BRIDGE
Medieval bridges, like old London Bridge (demolished in the 17th century), often contained shops and houses. The bridge itself was built in 1209, but the houses and shops were added later in a variety of materials and styles. London Bridge had stone buildings, wood-framed houses in the familiar "black-and-white" style, and other wood-framed buildings faced with plaster or wood paneling.

House covered with
weatherboarding
(wooden paneling)

Wooden supports hold
up buildings projecting
out over the river.

Stone arch

FACTS AND FIGURES
• Early medieval houses often had only two rooms – one for people, the other for animals.

• There were no chimneys in medieval houses, just a hole in the roof. Heat came from a central fire.

• In 1666, most of London's closely huddled wooden houses burned down in the Great Fire.

CASTLES

THE NOBILITY OF medieval Europe often lived in castles, which were military strongholds as well as homes. A castle was designed to withstand a siege. It was self-sufficient, with workshops, kitchens, stables, and storerooms. There was also a strong building, called a great tower, or keep.

Castle defense

Builders developed different ways of protecting their buildings from attack. These ranged from earthworks to strong stone towers and rings of stone curtain walls.

Motte

Bailey

ROCHESTER CASTLE, ENGLAND

Keep

MOTTE AND BAILEY
French warriors, known as the Normans, put up many wooden castles. They built a motte (earth mound) with a wooden tower. The bailey (adjoining courtyard) contained wooden huts for people and animals.

STONE CASTLE
In the 11th century, castles often had square keeps with thick walls. A keep held rooms for the lord and his household, a chapel, and storerooms.

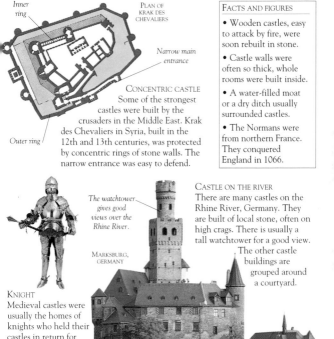

Inner ring

PLAN OF
KRAK DES
CHEVALIERS

Narrow main entrance

Outer ring

CONCENTRIC CASTLE

Some of the strongest castles were built by the crusaders in the Middle East. Krak des Chevaliers in Syria, built in the 12th and 13th centuries, was protected by concentric rings of stone walls. The narrow entrance was easy to defend.

FACTS AND FIGURES

• Wooden castles, easy to attack by fire, were soon rebuilt in stone.

• Castle walls were often so thick, whole rooms were built inside.

• A water-filled moat or a dry ditch usually surrounded castles.

• The Normans were from northern France. They conquered England in 1066.

CASTLE ON THE RIVER

There are many castles on the Rhine River, Germany. They are built of local stone, often on high crags. There is usually a tall watchtower for a good view. The other castle buildings are grouped around a courtyard.

The watchtower gives good views over the Rhine River.

MARKSBURG,
GERMANY

KNIGHT

Medieval castles were usually the homes of knights who held their castles in return for service to the king. This knight's armor dates from the 15th century.

Inside a castle

Take away one wall of a stone castle keep and you will see the main room where the lord and his family lived. This room was used for both sleeping and eating. Below this were storerooms, and above might be quarters for soldiers. Within the walls were additional small rooms, some of them containing simple lavatories called garderobes.

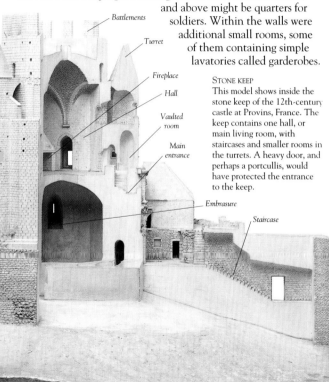

Battlements

Turret

Fireplace

Hall

Vaulted room

Main entrance

Embrasure

Staircase

STONE KEEP
This model shows inside the stone keep of the 12th-century castle at Provins, France. The keep contains one hall, or main living room, with staircases and smaller rooms in the turrets. A heavy door, and perhaps a portcullis, would have protected the entrance to the keep.

LOOPHOLES
Defenders fired through loopholes set in an embrasure (alcove). Arched openings were set at low levels. Cross-shaped holes were for arrows, circular holes for guns.

ARCHED   CROSS   CIRCULAR

DUNGEONS
Few castles served as prisons, and rooms now called "dungeons" were often simply storerooms. But when people were locked up in a castle, sturdy oak bars and thick stone walls ensured security.

GATEHOUSE, CAERPHILLY CASTLE, WALES

Machicolations

Loophole

Portcullis

CASTLE GATEHOUSE
The gatehouse was usually well defended. Protected by oak doors and a portcullis, defenders dropped missiles on enemies below through openings called machicolations.

Staircase

Courtyard

Motte

COURTYARD
Castle buildings were often grouped around a central courtyard. An open staircase rises beside the courtyard of this castle at Saumur in France.

ROMANESQUE

THE GRAND BUILDINGS of Western Europe in the early medieval period often imitated Roman architecture. Called Romanesque, this style used round arches, simple vaults, and, in some places, Corinthian capitals. Churches were often built to the Romans' basilica design. New features, such as façades with rows of arches and frontages with twin towers, were added.

Decorative arcading

LEANING TOWER OF PISA
This famous leaning tower was built as the bell tower for Pisa Cathedral in Italy. It is circled with decorative arches, called arcading, and leans about 16.4 ft (5 m) to one side.

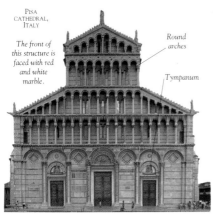

PISA CATHEDRAL, ITALY

The front of this structure is faced with red and white marble.

Round arches

Tympanum

PISA CATHEDRAL
The west front of Pisa Cathedral uses rounded arches similar to those on the tower. Larger arches surround the doors, each with a decorated semicircular tympanum above them.

ABBEY OF ST. FOI

A cutaway model of this French pilgrimage church shows how the aisles of Romanesque churches were often much lower than the central nave. An upper gallery, called a tribune, occupies the space above.

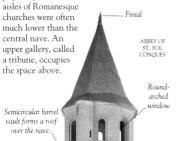

Finial

ABBEY OF ST. FOI, CONQUES

Round-arched window

Semicircular barrel vault forms a roof over the nave.

Tribune (elevated platform)

Nave

Side aisle

ST. MADELEINE

This church at Vezelay, France, has a typical Romanesque interior. The barrel vault, striped arches, and Corinthian columns are similar to those of the Romans.

FACTS AND FIGURES

• Simple wooden roofs were widely used.

• Some capitals had designs sculpted with biblical scenes.

• Bold carvings, such as zigzags, were used to decorate windows, arches, and doorways.

• Pisa's leaning tower moves about 0.043 in (1.1 mm) each year.

GOTHIC

THE 12TH CENTURY saw the emergence of the distinctive Gothic style. Features are pointed arches, large windows, stone tracery, stone vaulted ceilings, and flying buttresses. Many of Europe's finest churches are in this imposing yet delicate style.

CARVING BALLFLOWERS

Ballflowers are typical of 14th-century Gothic. Masons carved these in the sequence shown below. They may have a three-or four-leafed pattern.

LIMESTONE BLOCK   INITIAL CARVING   FINISHED BALLFLOWERS

FACTS AND FIGURES

• Gothic stained glass windows told Bible stories to those who could not read.

• In 1573, the 500-ft (150-m) spire of Beauvais Cathedral, Paris collapsed.

• Spires were built using scaffolding and wooden cranes.

• Notre Dame in Paris was built over a period of 170 years.

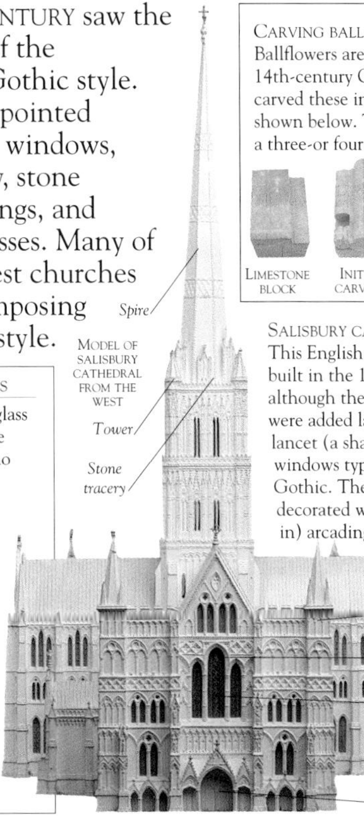

Spire

MODEL OF SALISBURY CATHEDRAL FROM THE WEST

Tower

Stone tracery

SALISBURY CATHEDRAL

This English cathedral was built in the 13th century, although the tower and spire were added later. It has simple lancet (a sharp, pointed arch) windows typical of early Gothic. The west front is decorated with blind (filled-in) arcading.

Blind arcading

Triple lancet window

Stained glass window

West doorway

CHURCH OF SAINTE-CHAPELLE
This church was built in Paris in the 13th century. It was built for the French royal family, and has the elaborate carved tracery typical of this later period. The apsidal (semicircular) east end of the church is a common feature of French Gothic buildings.

Gothic-style spire added in the 19th century

Interior decorated with blind arcading and statues of the apostles

Pinnacle

UPPER CHAPEL
The 16 windows of the upper chapel are a pictorial Bible, showing over 1,000 scenes from the Old and New Testaments.

Rose Window made up of 86 stained glass panels

MAIN PORTAL
You can clearly see the characteristic Gothic pointed arch in Sainte-Chapelle's main portal, or doorway.

Main portal

Lower chapel

Upper chapel, reserved for the royal family

Notre Dame

Almost 200 years in the making, Notre Dame Cathedral is a landmark not only in Paris, but in Gothic architecture. It has all the characteristic features of the Gothic style. The most striking feature is the elaborate west front with its two imposing towers and rose window. The west front contains the three main entrance doorways and is decorated with rows of statues.

GOTHIC WINDOWS

In the 12th century, Gothic windows were often simple lancets. These were paired in the 13th century to make two-light windows, which can be seen in Notre Dame. Later still, windows were filled with tracery. Two typical tracery styles were geometric and perpendicular.

LANCET

TWO-LIGHT WINDOW

GEOMETRIC TRACERY

PERPENDICULAR TRACERY

INTERIOR

Inside Notre Dame there is a long, tall nave. On either side of the nave are two aisles through which processions marched in medieval times. At the east end of the nave is a sanctuary (holy place) with stalls for the clergy. There are also numerous chapels where small-scale services and Masses for the dead were held. A large transept cuts across the nave at right angles to form the shape of a cross when the cathedral is viewed from above.

Notre Dame's towers are 226 ft (69 m) tall.

Gargoyles

West rose window

King's gallery

Main doorway

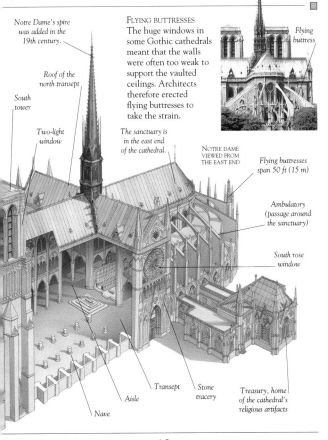

Notre Dame's spire was added in the 19th century.

FLYING BUTTRESSES
The huge windows in some Gothic cathedrals meant that the walls were often too weak to support the vaulted ceilings. Architects therefore erected flying buttresses to take the strain.

Flying buttress

Roof of the north transept

South tower

Two-light window

The sanctuary is in the east end of the cathedral.

NOTRE DAME VIEWED FROM THE EAST END

Flying buttresses span 50 ft (15 m)

Ambulatory (passage around the sanctuary)

South rose window

Transept

Stone tracery

Aisle

Nave

Treasury, home of the cathedral's religious artifacts

ISLAMIC ARCHITECTURE

MOSQUES AND TOMBS are usually the most important buildings in Islamic countries. They are decorated with abstract patterns, foliage motifs, and exquisite calligraphy from the Islamic sacred book, the Koran.

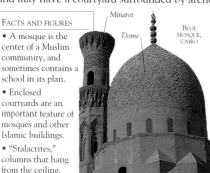

Ceramic tiles

Niche

Middle East and India

The Islamic faith spread rapidly in the 7th century, especially through the Middle East, southern Asia, and northern Africa. A mosque is a building for worship and group prayer. It contains a prayer hall, usually with a domed roof, and may have a courtyard surrounded by arches.

FACTS AND FIGURES

• A mosque is the center of a Muslim community, and sometimes contains a school in its plan.

• Enclosed courtyards are an important feature of mosques and other Islamic buildings.

• "Stalactites," columns that hang from the ceiling, are used in many Islamic buildings.

Minaret

Dome

BLUE MOSQUE, CAIRO

MIHRAB
Inside every mosque is a decorated niche called a mihrab. This indicates the direction of Mecca, the holy city of Islam.

BLUE MOSQUE
This mosque's large domed prayer hall and tall minaret are typical Islamic features. The minaret is used by a muezzin (an official) to call the faithful to prayer.

TAJ MAHAL
The marble walls of the Taj Mahal are delicately carved with a floral motif and inlaid with semiprecious stones.

PLAN OF THE TAJ MAHAL

1. ROYAL TOMB
2. PONDS
3. MOSQUE
4. RESTHOUSE
5. CANAL
6. GREAT GATEWAY

Minaret

PARADISE ON EARTH
This beautifully symmetrical building at Agra, India, is decorated with inscriptions from the Koran. The Mogul emperor, Shah Jehan, built it in the 17th century for his wife Mumtaz Mahal.

Plinth to raise the tomb above ground level

Dome of marble

TAJ MAHAL, AGRA, INDIA

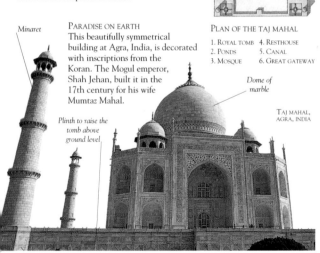

Islamic Spain

Spain was ruled by Muslims for several centuries during the medieval period. Known as the Moors, these people came from Syria and northern Africa, and their style of architecture was influenced by these areas. Their mosques and palaces have shady courtyards, forests of pillars, scalloped arches, and ornate plaster ceiling decorations.

One of 24 fortified towers

Hall of the Two Sisters

Scalloped arch

Ornate "stalactite" plasterwork

Horseshoe arch

Colonnade

GREAT MOSQUE

This mosque at Cordoba in Spain was begun in A.D.785. Its arches have alternating bands of brick and stone, giving a striped effect. The original arches were round, but horseshoe and scalloped arches followed.

ALHAMBRA

This palace-fortress was the last stronghold of the Moors in Granada, southern Spain. Inside its strong outer walls, colonnaded courtyards with fountains and covered walks offer shade from the hot sun. The luxurious rooms are richly decorated with stone carvings, mosaic tiles, and ornate plasterwork.

FORTIFIED PALACE

The Alhambra is positioned on the top of a hill and protected by its high red brick walls. It was built between 1238 and 1358 by Moorish princes.

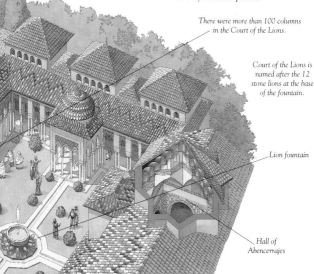

There were more than 100 columns in the Court of the Lions.

Court of the Lions is named after the 12 stone lions at the base of the fountain.

Lion fountain

Hall of Abencerrajes

INDIA

INDIA IS HOME TO A HOST of different cultures and religious influences, and has a diversity of building styles and techniques. Hinduism, with its many gods, and Jainism and Buddhism, with their emphasis on the search for enlightenment, have produced a variety of religious buildings. These range from domed-shaped Buddhist shrines (or stupas) to Jain and Hindu temples with pointed roofs.

Carved pillar

ELLURA TEMPLE OF ROCK
This Hindu temple is carved out of solid rock. From outside, the natural face of the cliff can be seen above the carvings of elephants and round pillars.

INSIDE ELLURA
Inside the Ellura temples, forests of pillars, carved roofs, and entire statues have been hewn out of the cliff. In some places the rock has been cut through to allow sunlight in.

DILWARRA JAIN TEMPLE

This sumptuous shrine at Mount Abu was built in the 10th century. The interior is of marble, which had to be brought to the site along a specially made sloping roadway. The roof is a shallow, intricately carved dome supported on pillars.

- The dome of a Buddhist stupa symbolizes the Universe.
- There are 34 rock-cut temples at Ellura alone.
- In Buddhist buildings, ornament often follows the lines of the structure.
- The Kailasanatha temple at Ellura is 277 ft (84 m) deep.

GREAT STUPA,
SANCHI

Dome

The four gates symbolize the winds.

GREAT STUPA

This building was originally at the heart of a Buddhist monastery. It is based on an earth mound. The original bricks on the outside were replaced by stone in c.150 B.C.

KHANDARIYA
MAHADEVA
TEMPLE,
INDIA

Ritual carvings

Conical tower

MOUNTAIN OF STONE

The huge, conical tower of this and similar Hindu temples has been compared to huge mountains of stone. In fact, they are intended to imitate the mythical Mount Meru, which is supposed to separate Heaven and Earth.

SOUTHEAST ASIA

TWO EARLY CIVILIZATIONS of Southeast Asia, the Sailendra of Java, and the Khmers of Cambodia, have left impressive evidence of their architecture, dating from the 9th to 13th centuries. In Cambodia, Hindu temple-cities were built to glorify the god-kings of the Khmer empire. The Buddhist stupas (shrines) of Java, by contrast, are designed to encourage meditation.

BOROBUDUR,
JAVA,
INDONESIA

BOROBUDUR
This 9th century Javanese stupa is built with gray volcanic stone. Statues of Buddha are present to encourage people to follow his path toward enlightenment.

STONE TERRACES
This building is a great mound with nine stone terraces. The lower terraces are decorated with relief carvings of the life of Buddha; the upper stories are plainer.

GUARDIAN OF ANGKOR WAT

Gate-guards like this one are set on the tall towers of this 12th-century temple in Cambodia. The Khmers believed the guards protected the shrine. The walls of the gallery are decorated with carved reliefs.

TEMPLE CITY

The Khmer kings built vast sandstone temples to be buried in. This temple at Angkor (the capital of the Khmer civilization) is built around courtyards and surrounded by moats. It is famous for its tall, conical towers.

Conical sandstone tower

Gallery richly decorated with reliefs

Portico

ANGKOR WAT, CAMBODIA

EARLY AMERICAN CIVILIZATIONS

SOME EARLY AMERICAN buildings still remain today.
The Maya flourished in Central America between
A.D. 200 and 1000; the Aztecs in Mexico in the
14th to 16th centuries; and the Incas in
Peru in the 15th and 16th centuries.

The Maya

The Maya were based in cities
around Mexico, Honduras,
and Guatemala. Their
most impressive
buildings were
pyramids consisting of
stone-covered earth mounds with
terracing, steps up the side, and
stone temples on top.

Inner core

Outer facing
of stone

The pyramid
consisted of nine
steep stone steps.

People could
stand on each
level.

ATLANTIC
OCEAN

The
Maya

PACIFIC
OCEAN

LOCATION OF THE MAYA
The Maya kingdom occupied
much of central America.

TEMPLE OF THE INSCRIPTIONS

This pyramid at Palenque in Mexico was built in the 7th century, and consists of a stepped mound of earth, faced with stone. Inside the pyramid is the tomb of the Mayan king Pacal. The temple on top has carved panels describing the events of the king's reign.

TEMPLE

CENTRAL PLAZA

The Temple of the Inscriptions stands in what was Palenque's central plaza, near the palace and other temples. Today, only this central area is visible. The other parts of the city are covered by dense rainforest.

Temple

Steps to tomb (blocked after the king's burial)

Outer steps to temple

King's tomb

Memorial slab

SECTION PULLED OUT FROM MAIN ARTWORK

FACTS AND FIGURES

• The Pyramid of the Sun at Teotihuacan is just over 200 ft (60 m) tall.

• Mayan pyramids were decorated with colored plaster.

• Some Mayan cities, such as Tikal, had populations of 40,000 to 50,000.

• Most Mayan pyramids are simple platforms for temples.

The Aztecs

For over a century, the Aztec people held power over Mexico. They built a large city called Tenochtitlán where Mexico City now stands. In the middle of the city was a walled compound that was the center of Aztec religion. The Aztecs practiced human sacrifice, believing that it pleased their gods. Their pyramidal temples were similar to those of the Mayan people.

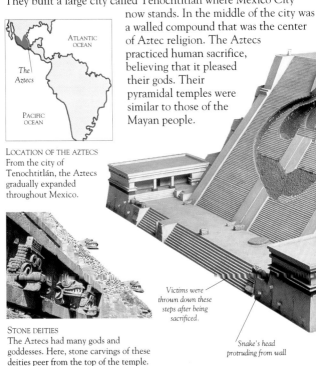

LOCATION OF THE AZTECS
From the city of Tenochtitlán, the Aztecs gradually expanded throughout Mexico.

STONE DEITIES
The Aztecs had many gods and goddesses. Here, stone carvings of these deities peer from the top of the temple.

Victims were thrown down these steps after being sacrificed.

Snake's head protruding from wall

Shrine to Tlaloc

Shrine to Huitzilopochtli

Sacrificial stone

1431
1454
1469
1390
1500

QUETZALCOATL
This image shows the feathered-serpent god, Quetzalcoatl. This was the god of self-sacrifice, and inventor of agriculture in Aztec myths.

The remains of five separate temples have been found on the same site.

Outer stone covering

GREAT TEMPLE AT TENOCHTITLAN
On top of this enormous stone pyramid stood twin shrines dedicated to Tlaloc, the god of rain, and Huitzilopochtli, the god of war. Beneath the outer stone "skin" of the pyramid, archaeologists have found a succession of smaller temples, covered as each new Aztec ruler built a bigger temple on the same site.

The Incas

South America's first great builders were the Incas, who established a large empire in the west of the continent during the 15th century. Their buildings were made of irregularly shaped stones which skilled stonemasons ground to fit together perfectly. These stone buildings still exist in their best-preserved city, Machu Picchu in Peru, and at the Inca capital of Cuzco.

ATLANTIC
OCEAN

The Inca

PACIFIC
OCEAN

LOCATION OF THE INCAS
The Inca Empire spread along the west coast of what is now Peru, and parts of Bolivia and Chile.

MACHU
PICCHU,
PERU

Farming
terraces

Central
plaza

MACHU PICCHU
Perched some 9,000 ft (3,150 m) above sea level, the ancient city of Machu Picchu is a stunning example of Inca building. The stone blocks of the stairs, linking its different levels, were cut so precisely that no mortar was required.

FORTRESS OF SACSAHUAMAN
This large fortress overlooks the city of Cuzco. It is built of massive stone blocks – some as big as 27 ft (8.2 m) high – which make up thick, zigzagging walls. The 0.3-mile (0.5-km) long building provided a secure refuge for the inhabitants of the Inca capital in troubled times.

Carved head

GATE OF THE SUN
Evidence of the high degree of skill attained by early South American stonemasons is borne by this gateway at the city of Tiahuanaco. Almost one thousand years old, it is cut from a single block of stone 10 ft (3 m) high. The carved head is probably a portrait of an Inca god.

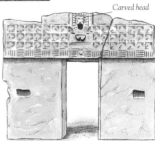

Houses   *Stone staircase*

TERRACED CITY
With its Temple of the Sun, palace, buildings of local stone, and terraces for crop growing, Machu Picchu is typical of an Inca provincial city. The buildings vary in shape, but most have trapezoidal (tapering) windows and doorways.

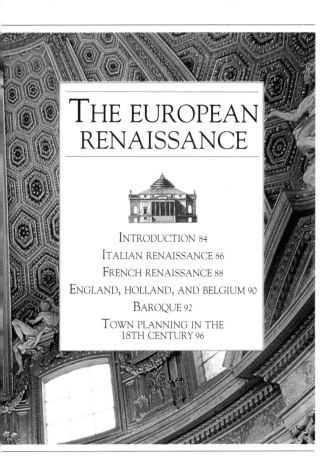

THE EUROPEAN RENAISSANCE

INTRODUCTION

ARCHITECTS IN 15TH-CENTURY Italy were the first to be influenced by the Renaissance, the intellectual movement that revived the learning and artistic styles of classical Greece and Rome. The influence of Italian Renaissance architecture, with its emphasis on symmetry and space, spread throughout Europe, ending in the extravagant decoration of early 18th-century baroque.

ITALIAN PALACE
Renaissance princes often lived in elegant classical palaces, decorated with details inspired by the buildings of ancient Greece and Rome. This one, the Palazzo del Te, was built by Giulio Romano in Mantua.

SCULPTORS' FRIEZE
In the Renaissance period, classical styles were revived in all the arts, not just architecture. Some architects, such as Bernini and Michelangelo, were also sculptors. Renaissance buildings were often adorned with elegant statues.

CHATEAU DE
CHENONCEAUX, FRANCE

FRENCH CHATEAU

While the Italians were building grand,
classical palaces, the French built
many less formally designed
châteaus, some of which include
fascinating features. This
château at Chenonceaux is
built partly on an arched
bridge over the River Cher.

*The deep-cut edges of the
stone produce an effect
called rustification.*

Doric
pilasters

IDEAL CITY

Italian Renaissance architects were fascinated by
the concept of the ideal city, planned from scratch
with beautiful vistas and imposing public buildings.
This plan for a city dates from 1552. Its circular
design was thought to be the perfect shape.

ITALIAN RENAISSANCE

RENAISSANCE architecture first appeared in the great Italian cities of Milan, Florence, Rome, and Venice. This new style of building based on the architecture of ancient Greece and Rome replaced the pointed-arched Gothic style with domed roofs and classical columns.

Central domed great hall rises the entire height of the villa.

VILLA CAPRA
This country house in Vicenza, also known as the Rotonda, was begun by Italian architect Andrea Palladio in 1552. Its plan is a perfect square, and the entrance portico is flanked by tall Ionic columns.

<table>
<tr><td>

FACTS AND FIGURES

• Florence was the first Italian city to reflect the influence of the Renaissance in its architecture.

• Italian Filippo Brunelleschi (1377-1446) was a very influential architect of the time.

• Michelangelo designed the dome of St. Peter's in Rome. It is 452 ft (135 m) high.

</td></tr>
</table>

PALAZZO PANDOLFINI
Italian painter and architect Raphael designed this palace in Florence in the early 16th century. The decoration is typical of its time. The windows have columns on either side and ornamental pediments.

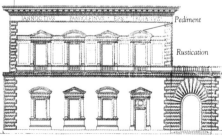

Pediment

Rustication

Colored marble

SANTA MARIA NOVELLA
Architect Leon Battista Alberti added an ornate west façade to this medieval church in Florence in 1456-70. It features a triangular pediment, Corinthian columns, and colored marble patterns.

The Tempietto marks the spot where St. Peter is thought to have died.

THE TEMPIETTO, ROME

Dome in shape of hemisphere

Doric column

DOORWAYS
Italian Renaissance doorways are often highly decorated and topped with a triangular pediment. Many have classical columns and carved stonework.

DOORWAY BY VIGNOLA

DOORWAY BY CARDI

DOORWAY BY SERLIO

DOMED CHAPEL
The Tempietto was built by Donato Bramante in 1502-10. It is modeled on a small round classical temple, with a dome and a ring of 16 Doric columns. The interior of this compact building is 15 ft (4.5 m) in diameter. It stands in the courtyard of San Pietro in Montorio, Rome.

Crypt

FRENCH RENAISSANCE

THE RENAISSANCE CAME later to France than it did to Italy. The first French Renaissance buildings were designed in the 16th century, and often show a combination of Gothic and classical details. Square-headed windows, steeply sloping roofs, and a restrained use of ornament are the trademarks of the style.

FRENCH WINDOWS
These were often square-headed, with swags (carvings of foliage or looped draperies). Curved-headed windows followed later.

EARLY WINDOW   MIDDLE WINDOW   LATE WINDOW

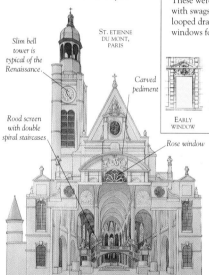

ST. ETIENNE DU MONT, PARIS

Slim bell tower is typical of the Renaissance.

Carved pediment

Rood screen with double spiral staircases

Rose window

PARISIAN CHURCH
French Renaissance buildings often show a mixture of styles. This church in Paris has a rose window, like those in some Gothic churches, and a delicate rood screen (the balcony holding the crucifix). The carved pediment is a typical Renaissance feature.

PALACE OF VERSAILLES

This enormous palace outside Paris was built for King Louis XIV by the architects Louis Le Vau and Jules Hardouin-Mansart. It is one of the biggest palaces ever built. Construction, which began in 1660, took almost 100 years. The staterooms and apartments are large enough to accommodate thousands of people.

The park facade was built between 1678-88.

FACTS AND FIGURES

• In its heyday Versailles was home to about 20,000 people.

• There are over 30 châteaus along the River Loire alone!

• Typical Renaissance interiors had carved wall paneling and painted ceilings.

• Renaissance details were often grafted onto traditional buildings.

CHAPELLE ROYALE

The interior of this chapel at Versailles is richly decorated with white marble, gilding, and baroque murals. The top floor was reserved for the royal family.

CHATEAU DE CHAMBORD, LOIRE

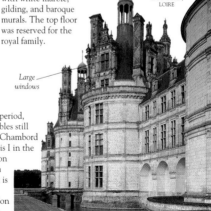

Large windows

PALACE FORTRESS

In the early Renaissance period, French monarchs and nobles still built castles. Château de Chambord was built for King François I in the 16th century. It is based on the medieval plan, with a keep and four towers, but is covered in Renaissance decoration. This decoration makes it look more like a palace than a fortress.

ENGLAND, HOLLAND, AND BELGIUM

LOCAL TRADITIONS influenced the Renaissance architecture of England, Holland, and Belgium. Quite unlike the style of Italy, buildings have large windows, ornate facades, and rich details, both inside and out. A stronger use of classical details, however, emerged during the 17th century.

ENGLAND
The English nobles of the late 16th century built a series of large country houses. Burghley in Northamptonshire is one of the grandest, with its dome-topped corner towers and gatehouse.

BURGHLEY HOUSE, ENGLAND

HARDWICK HALL
This Great Chamber is a superb example of a late 16th-century English interior. Its large windows, plaster friezes, tapestries, and wood paneling are all original.

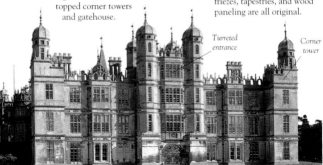

Turreted entrance

Corner tower

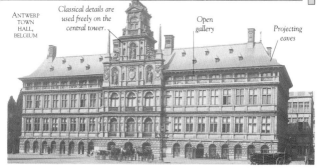

ANTWERP TOWN HALL, BELGIUM

Classical details are used freely on the central tower.

Open gallery

Projecting eaves

MAURITSHUIS, THE HAGUE, HOLLAND

Relief sculpture

Dutch steep roof

HOLLAND

This grand house in The Hague was built in c.1633. With its tall Ionic columns rising the full height of two stories, and its triangular pediments over the doors and windows, it is a good example of the Dutch style of the mid-17th century.

BELGIUM

Antwerp town hall is a typical early Renaissance building. It was designed by Cornelis Floris in 1561-66. Neat rows of windows give a regimented appearance, except for the elaborate tower in the center.

FACTS AND FIGURES

• Inigo Jones (1573-1652) brought the classical influence to English architecture.

• Lieven de Kay (1560-1627) and Hendrik de Keysert (1565-1621) created the Dutch style.

• Cornelis Floris (1504-75) was influential in Belgium.

BAROQUE

DURING THE 17TH CENTURY, a style emerged based on curved forms, rich materials, complex shapes, and dramatic lighting. It came to be called baroque, which originally meant irregular or misshapen. The first baroque buildings were seen in Italy, but the style spread to many other parts of Europe.

Italian baroque

The beginnings of baroque were in Rome, where architects Bernini and Borromini worked. Bernini began his career as a sculptor, and elements of his training can be seen in the baroque style. Statues are used as supports, and the curved walls appear to be molded.

DOME OF SAN CARLO ALLE QUATTRO FONTANE
This church in Rome was designed by Borromini. Its interior is dominated by a beautiful dome, which is coffered (recessed) using a variety of different shapes. It is lit by windows that are concealed from view and highlight the shapes in the dome.

BAROQUE DETAILS

Italian baroque buildings often have rich sculptural details. Niches, altarpieces, and façades are all common places for such statues.

ECSTASY OF ST. TERESA BY BERNINI

BUTTRESS WITH STATUE

SAN ANDREA AL QUIRINALE

Pink marble covers the interior walls of this church in Rome. It was designed by Bernini, demonstrating the liking of baroque architects for rich materials. Sculptures around the dome reach up to the central lantern, pointing toward the heavens.

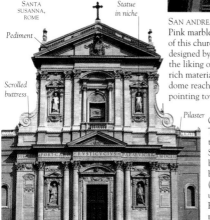

SANTA SUSANNA, ROME

Pediment

Scrolled buttress

Statue in niche

Pilaster

ORNATE FAÇADE

The scrolled brackets and the statues in niches mark Santa Susanna's façade as baroque. The spaces between the pilasters (half-columns) are varied, unlike the earlier Renaissance style which mostly used equally spaced rows of columns.

Northern baroque

The baroque style spread to northern Europe in the early 18th century. In England the result was a more severe, solid-looking style, with fewer curves but much of the rich detail found in European baroque. In Austria and Germany, interiors of great extravagance were produced, with lavish use of gilding and false-perspective ceiling paintings.

ST. GEORGE-IN-THE-EAST
Nicholas Hawksmoor designed several baroque churches in London. They are solid-looking buildings with heavy cornices, prominent triangular pediments, and striking steeples. Four pepper-pot lanterns add delicacy to this example.

ST. GEORGE-IN-THE-EAST, LONDON

Steeple

Cornice

Pediment

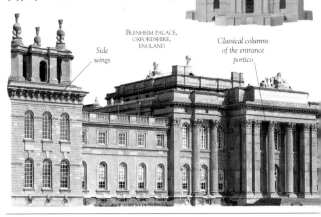

BLENHEIM PALACE, OXFORDSHIRE, ENGLAND

Side wings

Classical columns of the entrance portico

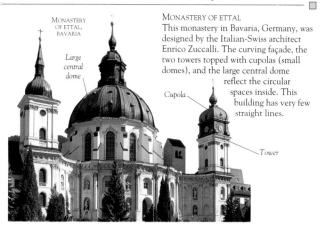

MONASTERY OF ETTAL, BAVARIA

Large central dome

Cupola

Tower

MONASTERY OF ETTAL

This monastery in Bavaria, Germany, was designed by the Italian-Swiss architect Enrico Zuccalli. The curving façade, the two towers topped with cupolas (small domes), and the large central dome reflect the circular spaces inside. This building has very few straight lines.

BENEDICTINE MONASTERY

Most of the inside surfaces of this baroque church in Melk, Austria, are decorated lavishly, from the bases of the fluted columns to the ceiling frescoes.

BLENHEIM PALACE

This Oxfordshire country house, designed by Sir John Vanbrugh, was a gift to the Duke of Marlborough. With its lofty rooms, four ornamented corner towers, and grand classical columns, it was built as a showpiece.

CHURCH WITHIN MONASTERY, MELK, AUSTRIA

TOWN PLANNING IN THE 18TH CENTURY

WHOLE NEW CITY DISTRICTS, or sometimes entire cities, were built from scratch in the 18th century. The reasons why this could happen varied. The Russian imperial city of St. Petersburg was created by Peter the Great as the new capital on the banks of the Neva River. The elegant streets of Bath were built to provide a holiday resort for the rich of England.

AERIAL VIEW OF BATH
John Wood I designed the Circus, a circular street of 33 houses. In each house, Doric, Ionic, and Corinthian orders are used for the first, second, and third floors respectively. His son, John Wood II, designed the nearby Royal Crescent and Assembly Rooms.

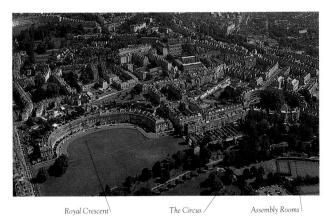

Royal Crescent   *The Circus*   *Assembly Rooms*

ROYAL CRESCENT

ROYAL CRESCENT, BATH, ENGLAND

Ionic column

The Royal Crescent in Bath is a great sweeping arc of 30 houses that stands on the crest of a hill. Ionic columns are doubled up at either end and in the center of the crescent, to give extra weight.

Balustraded parapet

Entablature

ST. PETERSBURG

This Russian city was founded in 1703 by Czar Peter the Great. He employed architects from Italy to create a lavish plan on the banks of the River Neva, with broad avenues radiating out from the central Admiralty and Winter Palace buildings. The south bank contains the historical center of the city; on the north are museums and a university.

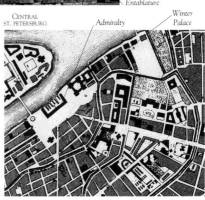

CENTRAL ST. PETERSBURG

Admiralty

Winter Palace

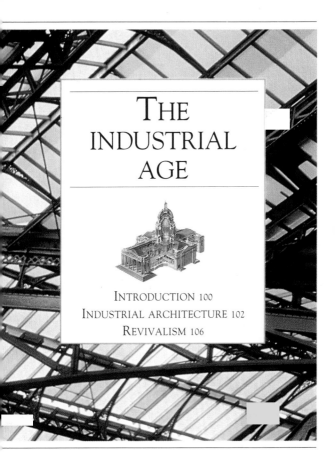

THE INDUSTRIAL AGE

INTRODUCTION

INNOVATIONS IN THE production of iron and steel, and the manufacture of textiles during the 18th century, forced many countries to move from an agricultural to an industrial economy. There was a need for different types of buildings. More people lived in cities, so large numbers of houses had to be built for them. Factories, too, were needed to house the new machinery for the manufacturing industries.

WATT'S STEAM ENGINE

STEAM ENGINE

The steam engine was a major driving force behind the Industrial Revolution, providing essential power to drive machinery. It was manufactured by Scottish engineer James Watt.

The bridge was assembled in 1779 from prefabricated components.

IRON BRIDGE, COALBROOKDALE, ENGLAND

Cast-iron rib

Stone abutment

IRON BRIDGE

Iron is a highly adaptable material, allowing new types of structures, such as the first iron bridge, to be built. The bridge has a 100-ft (30-m) span over the River Severn in England. A new town, called Ironbridge, grew up around it.

WORKERS' HOUSING

As industrialization spread, more and more people moved to the cities. They lived in small houses and went to work in the new factories. In England, the workers lived in long, straight streets of compact row houses.

RAILROAD WORKERS' COTTAGES, WILTSHIRE, ENGLAND

BLISS MILL, GLOUCESTERSHIRE, ENGLAND

Built in 1872, this mill has the characteristic tall chimney.

Rows of windows provide optimum light.

PLACE OF WORK

The 18th and 19th centuries were great eras of factory building. Inside, wide floors, often supported by iron columns, housed the machinery connected by drive belts to a steam engine. The outer walls were of brick, and many had a tall chimney.

FACTS AND FIGURES

• The first steam-powered loom appeared in 1787.

• Gas lighting appeared in *c*.1800.

• New types of buildings, such as warehouses and railroad stations, sprang up.

• Built in less than a year, London's Crystal Palace had a staggering 3,300 iron columns.

INDUSTRIAL ARCHITECTURE

AS INDUSTRIALIZATION SPREAD, iron became more widely available. Builders recognized that iron made building quicker and easier. If standard-length columns and beams were used, any number could be brought to the site and rapidly bolted together.

Buildings for industry

The rise of industry brought with it a demand for factories to house large machines and hundreds of workers, and for vast warehouses in which goods could be stored. Such buildings required large, uninterrupted floor areas. Brick or stone walls with slim iron columns provided the solution.

Venetian windows

FACTS AND FIGURES

• Iron smelting first began in *c*.1500 B.C.

• Steel is a modified form of iron with great strength and flexibility.

• The Eiffel Tower is 6 in (15 cm) taller on hot days when the iron structure expands.

• James Watt pioneered the steam engine and metal-framed buildings.

MILL

Industrial buildings of the 18th and 19th centuries often conceal an iron structure inside a skin of brick. The white quoins (corner stones) and the Venetian windows in this English cotton mill recall Renaissance buildings.

Iron tie rod

Brick vault

Iron column

Iron beam

Iron lattice window

FLAX-SPINNING MILL
This mill in Shrewsbury, England, was built in 1796. It has a skeleton of cast-iron columns, beams, and rods. Iron is also used for the large lattice-framed windows. The outside of the building is walled in brick. Each floor has a brick-vaulted ceiling to cut down the risk of fire.

OFFICE BUILDING
In the US, architects used iron on the outside of buildings. This office building in Philadelphia uses iron and glass to produce an Italian Renaissance effect.

PUMPING STATION
This London pumping station was built in 1865-68. Joseph Bazalgette used ornate iron arches, brackets, and walkways in this "industrial cathedral."

SMYTHE BUILDING, PHILADELPHIA.

ABBEY MILLS PUMPING STATION, LONDON, ENGLAND

New materials and structures

Spurred on by the need for new buildings, such as large railway stations and exhibition halls, 19th-century architects and engineers began to experiment with new ways of building with iron and steel. They created structures in which the skeleton of steel is the main feature. Steel frameworks could span vast interiors, and enabled very tall buildings to be constructed for the first time. These huge buildings could also be erected at great speed.

LIVERPOOL ST. STATION
Steel has greater tensile strength than iron and is an ideal material for the great arched train sheds that cover the platforms of major railroad stations. This station in London was built in 1874-5.

CRYSTAL PALACE
Built for the Great Exhibition of 1851, Paxton's Crystal Palace was constructed of prefabricated cast iron parts and sheets of glass, in some 22 weeks. After the exhibition, the entire 1,851-ft (564-m) building was taken apart and moved to another site.

CRYSTAL PALACE, LONDON

The Crystal Fountain

Living elm trees left standing inside

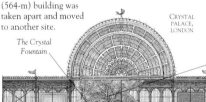

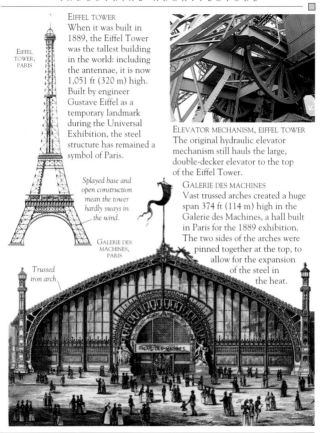

EIFFEL TOWER

When it was built in 1889, the Eiffel Tower was the tallest building in the world: including the antennae, it is now 1,051 ft (320 m) high. Built by engineer Gustave Eiffel as a temporary landmark during the Universal Exhibition, the steel structure has remained a symbol of Paris.

EIFFEL TOWER, PARIS

Splayed base and open construction mean the tower hardly sways in the wind.

ELEVATOR MECHANISM, EIFFEL TOWER

The original hydraulic elevator mechanism still hauls the large, double-decker elevator to the top of the Eiffel Tower.

GALERIE DES MACHINES

Vast trussed arches created a huge span 374 ft (114 m) high in the Galerie des Machines, a hall built in Paris for the 1889 exhibition. The two sides of the arches were pinned together at the top, to allow for the expansion of the steel in the heat.

GALERIE DES MACHINES, PARIS

Trussed iron arch

PALAIS DES MACHINES

REVIVALISM

IN THE 18TH AND 19TH centuries, architects began to revive ancient styles of architecture. First they looked to ancient Greece and Rome, designing buildings that looked like classical temples. Later they revived the medieval Gothic style.

The classical revival

Interest in ancient Greece increased in the 18th century, resulting in a fashion for buildings in the Greek style that lasted into the 19th century. Buildings often featured imposing porticos (porches) with massive columns.

ALL SOUL'S CHURCH, LANGHAM PLACE
This London church was built by John Nash in 1822-25. The circular portico features Ionic and Corinthian columns.

FACTS AND FIGURES

• The dome of the Capitol Building is 98 ft (30 m) wide.

• French architects were influenced by ancient buildings of Rome.

• British architects preferred the style of ancient Greece.

• The spires of Cologne Cathedral (1842-80) are 515 ft (157 m) high.

CAPITOL BUILDING, US

CAPITOL BUILDING
This famous structure in Washington, DC, was rebuilt several times between 1793 and 1867. The huge dome is made mainly of cast iron.

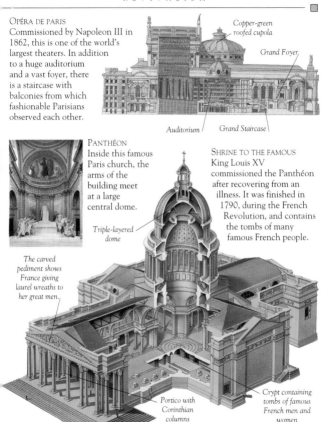

OPÉRA DE PARIS
Commissioned by Napoleon III in 1862, this is one of the world's largest theaters. In addition to a huge auditorium and a vast foyer, there is a staircase with balconies from which fashionable Parisians observed each other.

Copper-green roofed cupola

Grand Foyer

Auditorium

Grand Staircase

PANTHÉON
Inside this famous Paris church, the arms of the building meet at a large central dome.

Triple-layered dome

The carved pediment shows France giving laurel wreaths to her great men.

SHRINE TO THE FAMOUS
King Louis XV commissioned the Panthéon after recovering from an illness. It was finished in 1790, during the French Revolution, and contains the tombs of many famous French people.

Portico with Corinthian columns

Crypt containing tombs of famous French men and women

Gothic revival

During the 18th century, there was a reaction against the serious classicism of Greek revival buildings, and some architects began to build in an imitation of medieval Gothic. The first Gothic revival buildings were country houses, that used Gothic motifs with wit and delicacy. But by the 19th century, the Gothic revival became more entrenched as the style was used mostly for churches and cathedrals.

ST. JOHN THE DIVINE, NEW YORK

Position of planned central tower

Pulpit

The Rose Window was completed in 1933.

The portals of the West Front are adorned with fine stone carvings.

REVIVAL CATHEDRAL
New York's St. John the Divine was begun in 1892, and is still unfinished. It already boasts many features typical of large medieval churches – pointed arches, flying buttresses, and an ornate west front with a rose window. Twin west towers, and a taller central tower, are planned.

Pointed arches

Ogee moldings

COUNTRY HOUSE
This 18th-century English house in Gloucestershire has an elegant porch, patterned windows, and plain castlelike battlements.

LACOCK ABBEY
The elegant great hall of this English country house has windows, with ogee (double-curved) moldings, and a flower-shaped window typical of 18th-century Gothic revival buildings.

KEBLE COLLEGE, OXFORD
William Butterfield designed this with the chapel, hall, and students' rooms set around a quadrangle. It is constructed in a dazzling striped red, gray, and yellow pattern called polychrome.

ORIENTAL REVIVAL
There was a fashion in 19th-century England for imitating oriental buildings. The Royal Pavilion, Brighton, summer house of the Prince Regent, was designed in a mixture of Chinese and Indian styles by John Nash.

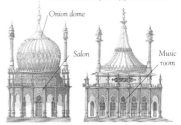

Onion dome

Salon

Music room

DETAILS OF ROYAL PAVILION, BRIGHTON

MODERN ARCHITECTURE

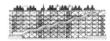

INTRODUCTION

ARCHITECTS BEGAN TO TURN AWAY from the old styles at the end of the 19th century. They were influenced by the availability of new materials, such as reinforced concrete, and new techniques of construction. A simple, more functional form evolved, and as it spread came to be known as the International Style.

1930s CAR
Increasingly in the 20th century, architects have drawn on fields outside building for their designs. The chrome-plated interiors of some Art Deco buildings were influenced by the sleek, stylish cars of the time – symbols of a new modern era.

FACTS AND FIGURES
• The term "Modern Architecture" caught on after an exhibition in New York in 1932.
• The Dutch De Stijl group was influenced by abstract and cubist art.
• The Louisiana Superdome in New Orleans has a dome 273 ft (82 m) tall.
• Chicago's Sears Tower, built in 1974, is still the world's tallest building.

HOUSING PLAN AT KIEFHOCK, HOLLAND

Oud planned every internal detail of these compact houses.

WORKERS' HOUSING
The Dutch architect J.J.P. Oud designed modern housing for ordinary people. These workers' houses, designed in the 1920s, have symmetrical layouts, simple lines, white walls, and minimal ornament typical of early 20th-century buildings.

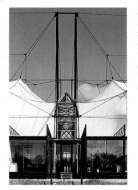

SCHLUMBERGER RESEARCH INSTITUTE
Architect Michael Hopkins came up with a novel design for this building, which houses offices and laboratories. Steel masts and cables tower above a floor of steel and glass. These support a fabric roof, making the building look like a gigantic tent billowing above the surrounding, flat countryside.

MONTREAL EXPO 67 DOME
American inventor and designer Richard Buckminster Fuller created the geodesic dome as a way of enclosing a large space in a structure with a relatively small surface area. These strong but lightweight domes have proved useful for factories and exhibitions. Materials as diverse as bamboo, plastic, and cardboard can be used to form the framework.

This dome is 200 ft (60 m) high.

US PAVILION AT MONTREAL'S EXPO 67

Interlocking steel struts

Plexiglass panels

THE ROOTS OF MODERN ARCHITECTURE

AT THE TURN of the century, fresh approaches to architecture began to emerge: the strong, simple work of the German Peter Behrens; the elegant buildings of Scotsman Charles Rennie Mackintosh; and the lavish style of the Art Nouveau movement.

A.E.G. TURBINE BUILDING
Peter Behrens designed this Berlin factory in 1908-9. Its curving corners and sloping glass walls make the factory both elegant and functional.

RED HOUSE
This house was built by Philip Webb for designer and writer William Morris in 1859. It mixes Gothic details, such as pointed arches, with later features, like sash windows. This style became known as Arts and Crafts.

RED HOUSE,
BEXLEYHEATH,
ENGLAND

Gothic-style pointed window

Rectangular sash window

THE LIBRARY
This is the school's most striking room. There are no curves in its design. Instead, rows of rectangular pillars and beams support the surrounding balcony.

GLASGOW SCHOOL OF ART
This highly original building was designed in 1896 by Charles Rennie Mackintosh. Its entrance shows how Mackintosh combined two different styles: elements of a traditional building are mixed with gentle curves influenced by the Art Nouveau movement.

THE EXTERIOR
The Glasgow School of Art took some 12 years to build. It combines traditional materials, such as stone, with a bold use of metal in the strong, gridlike lines of the windows. These windows flood the upper level studios with light. The west wing, added in 1907-9, has tall oriel (projecting) windows.

Strong gridlike windows

FACTS AND FIGURES
• Chairs designed by Mackintosh are still manufactured today.

• The Red House was Philip Webb's first commission.

• Behrens was also a teacher whose pupils included Le Corbusier and Mies van der Rohe.

• Mackintosh's work was more famous in Europe than in Britain.

ART NOUVEAU

WITH ITS FLOWING LINES and curves, the style that became known as Art Nouveau (new art) was created by a group of architects and designers at the end of the 19th century. Art Nouveau flourished briefly in France, Scotland, and Belgium, home of one of its most famous architects, Victor Horta.

Ornate roofs and spires adorned by mosaics.

HOUSE IN PARC GUELL, BARCELONA, SPAIN

CASA MILA, AN APARTMENT BUILDING DESIGNED BY GAUDI

ANTONI GAUDI

The Catalan architect Antoni Gaudí designed many buildings in his native Barcelona. His work ranged from houses and apartment buildings to a cathedral and a city park, Parc Guell. Gaudí's buildings are full of curves; in some, even the rooms have curved walls. Many are decorated with brilliant mosaics.

PARIS MÉTRO ENTRANCE

Many of the station entrances for the newly built Paris Métro were designed by Art Nouveau architect Hector Guimard. These designs featured amber lights, wrought-iron arches, and railings decorated with whiplash curves.

ENTRANCE TO LES ABBESSES STATION, PARIS

HOUSE INTERIOR

Every detail in the house was designed by Horta, including the marble columns, mosaic floors, and cast-iron radiators.

ART NOUVEAU HOUSE

The Belgian architect Victor Horta designed Van Eetvelde House in Brussels for a rich baron. The rooms are arranged around a central octagonal hall. Glass doors lead from the hall to the two main reception rooms – the salon and the dining room.

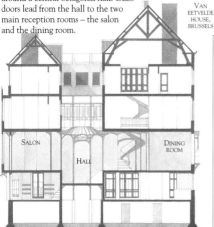

VAN EETVELDE HOUSE, BRUSSELS

SALON

HALL

DINING ROOM

FACTS AND FIGURES

• Art Nouveau got its name from a French art gallery, opened in 1895.

• Another name for the style was Style Nouille ("noodle style").

• A less ornate version of Art Nouveau developed in Scotland and Vienna.

• The glassware of Emile Gallé (1846-1904) was a product of Art Nouveau.

• Gaudí's cathedral in Barcelona, begun in 1883, is still being built.

CHICAGO

AFTER A FIRE devastated the city in 1871, Chicago rose high from the ashes. The first skyscrapers were built here, and architects such as Louis Sullivan and Dankmar Adler pioneered new building styles. Frank Lloyd Wright worked in Sullivan's office and would later design stunning buildings of his own.

CARSON, PIRIE, SCOTT DEPARTMENT STORE
The two lower floors of this Chicago store, built in 1899-1904, are faced with Sullivan's feathery cast-iron work.

FISHER BUILDING
Daniel H. Burnham and John W. Root designed several tall buildings in Chicago in the late 19th century. The Fisher Building is a steel-framed structure, built in 1897.

ROBIE HOUSE
This is one of the "prairie houses" designed by Frank Lloyd Wright. It was built in 1907-9. The low, horizontal lines and shallow, overhanging roofs are two of his hallmarks.

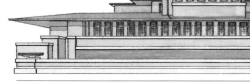

FACTS AND FIGURES

• Chicago expanded quickly after 1852, when the railroad first reached the city from the East.

• The Chicago fire destroyed one third of the city. Afterward, building regulations were changed to allow multistory structures.

• Some of the first apartment houses were built in Chicago.

AUDITORIUM BUILDING
This building by Sullivan and Adler was designed to contain an opera house, offices, and a hotel. It is a tall building for its time (1886-9), but it still makes use of traditional, load-bearing walls.

Load-bearing walls

845/860 LAKESHORE DRIVE
By 1949, architect Ludwig Mies van der Rohe had brought a very different style of skyscraper to Chicago. These apartment buildings are based on a steel framework, that is filled with glass.

The steel framework is visible from the outside.

THE INTERNATIONAL STYLE

DURING THE 1920s, architects began to build in a style that owed little to the past. They created tall glass-and-steel towers, white concrete houses with flat roofs and long strips of windows, and buildings with no additional and unnecessary decoration. These features are typical of the International Style of architecture, which began in Europe and spread to become the dominant style in cities of the United States.

BAUHAUS, DESSAU, GERMANY

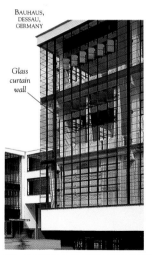

Glass curtain wall

CONCERT HALL
Finnish architect Alvar Aalto continued to design buildings in the International Style well into the mid-20th century. This concert hall in Helsinki, built in 1958, has curving concrete walls.

BAUHAUS
The Bauhaus was the most influential school of design of the early 20th century. Its buildings at Dessau, with their glass walls revealing a structure of steel and concrete, were designed by the director Walter Gropius in 1925-6.

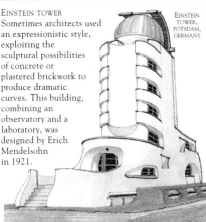

EINSTEIN TOWER, POTSDAM, GERMANY

EINSTEIN TOWER
Sometimes architects used an expressionistic style, exploiting the sculptural possibilities of concrete or plastered brickwork to produce dramatic curves. This building, combining an observatory and a laboratory, was designed by Erich Mendelsohn in 1921.

FACTS AND FIGURES
- Bauhaus students learned crafts as well as architecture.
- The Bauhaus closed in 1932, and many teachers went to America.
- A "New Bauhaus" was created in Chicago, Illinois, in 1937.
- A Dutch magazine called De Stijl (meaning "the style") gave its name to the movement.

Clock tower

HILVERSUM TOWN HALL
The architect Willem Dudok, who was influenced by the Dutch "De Stijl" group of artists, designed this town hall. It was completed in 1934. The De Stijl group produced buildings with plain white walls, carefully arranged windows, and details such as colored tiles.

TOWN HALL, HILVERSUM, HOLLAND

The projecting eaves appear to be unsupported.

The bands of low windows reflect the influence of Frank Lloyd Wright.

ART DECO

A RICHLY DECORATED style of architecture emerged in Europe and the United States during the 1920s. It was launched in France and became known as Art Deco (Arts Décoratifs). The style had a look of sleek elegance. Art Deco buildings often have rounded streamlined edges, sunbursts, and Egyptian motifs.

Arched sunburst

CHRYSLER SPIRE SUNBURST
The semicircular sunbursts of the Chrysler spire are typical of the Art Deco style. This close-up shows them in detail.

CHRYSLER BUILDING
The Chrysler Building is a 1,047-ft-high (319-m) office building in New York. It was built in 1928-30 by William van Alen. The steel-and-concrete skyscraper has a striking, tapering spire with sunbursts.

ELEVATOR DOORS
The Chrysler interior has lavish details such as elevator doors elegantly inlaid with wood and brass.

HOOVER FACTORY

The white walls, metal-framed windows, and striped corners and cornices of this factory make it one of the finest examples of English Art Deco. It was built in London in 1932-8 by Wallis Gilbert and Partners. Art Deco styles revolutionized industrial architecture.

Tapering window

WINDOW DETAILS

More unusual window shapes, including quarter-circles, are used on this corner of the factory. The tapering shape of the large window is a feature of Art Deco architecture.

HOOVER FACTORY, LONDON

Striped cornices

Pale green details

HOOVER DOORWAY DETAIL

The elaborate tiled and painted decoration above the doorway is influenced by the buildings of ancient Egypt. The pale green color of the window frames, also popular for roof tiles in this period, is repeated here.

DOORWAY DETAIL

HOOVER BUILDING

SKYSCRAPERS

TALL, METAL-FRAMED buildings soaring to the clouds are usually called skyscrapers. The first, the 10-story Chicago Home Insurance Building, was built in 1883. Safe passenger elevators and better steel structures allowed architects to build higher and higher.

TV mast

Observation tower

FLATIRON BUILDING
People thought that this building in New York would fall down when it was built in 1902. The triangular skyscraper has 21 stories, but its narrow corner is only 6 ft (185 cm) wide.

Limestone and granite facing

Art Deco decoration

EMPIRE STATE BUILDING, NEW YORK

EMPIRE STATE BUILDING
This building was the tallest in the world when it was erected in 1931. It has a steel frame, lined with bricks, and is faced with stone and aluminum panels. The 1,250-ft (381-m) skyscraper was built to a prefabricated design, and took only 15 months to complete.

NEW YORK SKYSCRAPER DETAILS

The Woolworth Building (1913) has a cathedral-like spire; the 1930's General Electric Building an Art Deco crown. The World Trade Center (1971) has less ornate detailing.

WOOLWORTH BUILDING

GENERAL ELECTRIC BUILDING

WORLD TRADE CENTER

CENTURY TOWER, TOKYO

Braced framework

WALL OF GLASS

This skyscraper was designed by German architect Mies van der Rohe in the 1950s. Its elegance is heightened by the use of high-quality materials – bronze, marble, and gray-tinted glass.

SEAGRAM BUILDING, NEW YORK

TWIN TOWERS

Sir Norman Foster's Century Tower has two towers (of 19 and 21 stories) linked by a central atrium that floods the building with light. There is a striking braced framework, visible from the outside.

GREAT MODERN HOUSES

SOME OF THE MOST famous modern buildings are unique houses, which give an architect the chance to create something new. The best examples from the middle of the 20th century show striking uses of materials (especially concrete and glass), dramatic placement of the house in its surroundings, and unusual interior plans.

FALLINGWATER

Fallingwater is perched above a waterfall in Pennsylvania. Frank Lloyd Wright designed the house in the 1930s. It has thick stone walls, sweeping roofs and dramatically projecting balconies.

FARNSWORTH HOUSE

This house was built in the 1940s by Mies van der Rohe. Its design is a simple glass box supported by elegant steel beams. The huge windows allow the inside and outside spaces to merge. The single living area is divided into two by a huge closet.

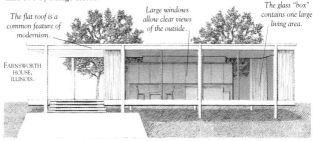

The flat roof is a common feature of modernism.

Large windows allow clear views of the outside.

The glass "box" contains one large living area.

FARNSWORTH HOUSE, ILLINOIS.

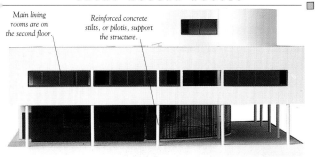

Main living rooms are on the second floor.

Reinforced concrete stilts, or pilotis, support the structure.

OVERHEAD VIEW, VILLA SAVOYE

The first floor of this house is taken up by garages, and the main living rooms are on the floor above. A gentle ramp rises through the center of the house to terraces on the upper floors. Concrete screens give privacy and shelter.

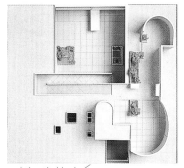

Lightweight slabs of concrete form the walls.

VILLA SAVOYE

This house in Poissy, France, was built by Le Corbusier in 1929-31. It is constructed of lightweight concrete slabs and rendered (plastered) brickwork. The white walls and columns reflect the elegance of classical Greece.

> ### FACTS AND FIGURES
>
> • Mies van der Rohe's building philosophy was "Less is more."
>
> • Frank Lloyd Wright believed that a building should "grow" out of the earth like a natural organism.
>
> • Le Corbusier is quoted as saying, "A house is a machine for living in."

CONTEMPORARY ARCHITECTURE

MODERN BUILDINGS reflect the freedom of design that new materials and better technology bring. Some architects continue to design in the International Style, building tall steel-and-glass office buildings and apartment houses. Many have explored the sculptural qualities of concrete, and others have turned buildings inside out, placing pipes, air-conditioning, and services on the outside.

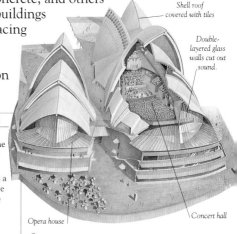

Shell roof covered with tiles

Double-layered glass walls cut sound.

Opera house

Concert hall

FACTS AND FIGURES

• A building that reflects its use on the outside is known as "functionalist."

• Postmodernism is a colorful, imaginative style of architecture that rejects simple modernist ideals.

• Philip Johnson's AT&T Headquarters in New York was the first famous postmodern building.

SYDNEY OPERA HOUSE
The Danish architect Jørn Utzon designed this structure. It contains both a large concert hall and an opera house. It has stunning, shell-like roofs made of concrete ribs covered with gleaming ceramic tiles.

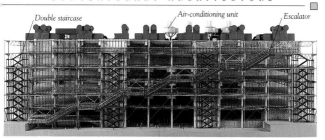

Double staircase   Air-conditioning unit   Escalator

CENTRE GEORGES POMPIDOU, PARIS

CENTRE GEORGES POMPIDOU

Architects Richard Rogers and Renzo Piano put all the services – water pipes, stairways, air-conditioning, and elevators – on the outside of this building. This allows for vast, uninterrupted exhibition areas inside.

POMPIDOU EXTERIOR
The building is crisscrossed by steel lattice beams. Pipes run up the outsides.

NOTRE DAME DU HAUT, RONCHAMP

The roof has a metal framework

NOTRE DAME DU HAUT

This French church was designed by Le Corbusier. The curved, concrete walls are pierced with small stained glass windows to throw pools of colored light into the white interior. The roof is metal and concrete.

20TH-CENTURY CITIES

FROM IMPRESSIVE CENTERS of government to housing for ordinary people in pleasant surroundings, city planning continues to fascinate 20th-century architects. Planned new towns, complete with housing, roads, schools, and services, were first built in England at the turn of the century. Today, planned communities are found across the world.

BOURNVILLE GARDEN CITY
This town in England was built by a Quaker chocolate manufacturer to house his workers. The houses had generous gardens, so that the occupants could grow food and live in a "green" environment.

Tree-lined roads were built around a central green with shops.

OLD PARLIAMENT
HOUSE, CANBERRA

Central meeting hall

CANBERRA

Australia's specially built capital was begun in
1913 to a design by Walter Burley Griffin. The
city is zoned, with different areas for shops,
houses, government offices, and so on. Many of
the roads radiate out from circular parks,
like the spokes of a wheel. The new
Parliament House was added in 1988.

*The twin towers contain
the administrative offices.*

NATIONAL CONGRESS
BUILDING,
BRASILIA

*The reversed dome of the
Chamber of Deputies reflects
Brasilia's evening sunshine.*

BRASILIA

Planned on a rural site by Lúcio Costa, Brazil's modern
capital features buildings designed by Oscar Niemeyer.
These structures, like the Congress Building shown
here, are outstanding, but the city had little low-cost
housing, forcing people out into the outskirts.

FACTS AND FIGURES

• Seen from the air,
Brasilia appears to
be planned in the
shape of an aircraft.

• Houses in
Bournville Garden
City had sunken
baths – but they
were in the
kitchen!

• Le Corbusier and
Tony Garnier both
produced plans for
ideal cities, but these
were never built.

THE FUTURE

ALMOST ANYTHING may be possible in future buildings, from energy-efficient designs to services controlled by computer. Natural energy sources such as wind power and solar heating will be used where the climate allows, and buildings will be insulated with new materials to save energy.

The building is about half a mile (1 km) long.

N.M.B. BANK
This is thought to be the world's most energy-efficient building. Glazed panels on the roof collect solar energy for heating and insulated water tanks in the basement recycle waste heat from equipment within the building. The walls are insulated with mineral fiber.

N.M.B. BANK, NEAR AMSTERDAM, HOLLAND

Pentagonal glazed areas collect solar energy.

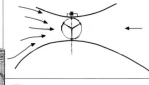

TURBINE TOWER

A series of turbines is incorporated into this design, so that the building's energy needs can be met by wind power. In winter, sun is let in to warm the tower, and a heat-exchange system heats the cool air. The building absorbs and stores the extra heat generated in the summer.

The building is shaped to encourage the wind to pass through the turbines.

WIND TESTING

A wind tunnel was used to test models of the building and its turbines. This allowed the architects to work out the best shape for both tower and turbines, taking into account the local wind speeds and the effect of nearby buildings on the speed and direction of the wind.

TURBINE TOWER,
PLANNED FOR
TOKYO, JAPAN

Wind turbine

Service tower

FACTS AND FIGURES

• Sir Norman Foster's Millennium Tower, planned for Tokyo, will soar to 2,515 ft (762 m).

• The United States is planning a permanent space station, *Freedom*.

• Computer-controlled mechanisms will protect future buildings from earthquake damage.

• Materials that use less energy to manufacture will be used more frequently in the future.

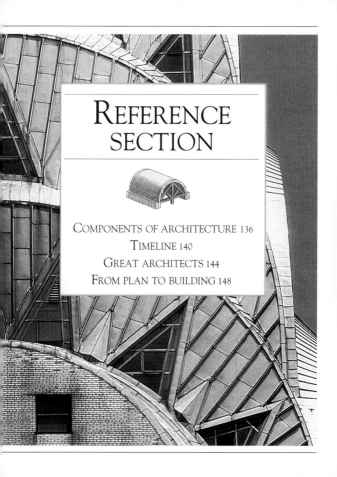

REFERENCE SECTION

COMPONENTS OF ARCHITECTURE

THE DETAILS – doors, windows, and arches – can tell us a lot about a building. As structures and fashions change over the years, these features can help to date a building. There are also local variations which are revealed in these key elements.

ARCHES

Large buildings, such as churches and cathedrals, often have many arches, providing clues to the age of a building. Perhaps the most outstanding innovation was the pointed arch in Europe in the 11th century, which paved the way for the Gothic style.

BASKET ARCH
This arch was used in Romanesque buildings up to the 11th century.

LANCET ARCH
This type of slender, pointed arch was used in the later 11th and 12th centuries.

TREFOIL ARCH
This more ornate type of Gothic arch appeared in the 14th century.

TUDOR ARCH
In Britain in the 16th century, arches were often built to this flatter design.

WINDOWS

With the increasing availability of large, flat sheets of clear glass, windows have changed radically over the centuries. In early medieval times, windows often had no glass and were very small. Today, the entire exterior of a building may be glazed.

ANGLO-SAXON WINDOW
Windows in the 10th and 11th centuries were often tiny, unglazed openings.

ROMANESQUE WINDOW
The semicircular head and columns are typical of the Byzantine and Romanesque.

BAROQUE WINDOW
This oeil de boeuf (ox eye) window was used in the 17th and 18th centuries.

MODERN WINDOWS
Plate glass and metal frames allowed the 20th-century "wall of glass."

DOORWAYS

These show a similar development to windows, but often have additional ornament on the jambs (sides) and above the door. They vary in size according to the importance of the building – grand structures, such as churches, cathedrals, and public buildings, usually have large, ornate doorways with decorative carving.

ROMANESQUE DOORWAY
This Romanesque doorway from the early 12th century has recessed semicircular arches.

GOTHIC DOORWAY
Builders in the 13th century used recessed arches, but by then they had become pointed.

ANCIENT GREEK DOORWAY
The Greeks made little use of arches, so their doorways have a rectangular shape.

RENAISSANCE DOORWAY
Renaissance architects revived the rectangular shape of ancient Greece and Rome.

ANGLO-SAXON DOORWAY
The Saxons often used triangular openings for doorways. The decoration was usually plain.

ART NOUVEAU DOORWAY
At the end of the 19th century, architects experimented with shapes like this elipsoid.

VAULTS

A simple barrel vault is an arched covering in stone or brick – it always looked the same, and was difficult to build strongly in a wide building. The introduction of the pointed arch, together with intersecting ribs, allowed for stronger, wider vaults.

GROIN VAULT
Two intersecting barrel vaults were joined with groins in an X-shape.

RIB VAULT
Gothic builders developed the rib vault, using pointed arches in rectangular spaces.

BARREL VAULT
A simple Romanesque vault, this creates a semi-circular tunnel effect.

FAN VAULT
This ornate version of the rib vault was introduced in the late medieval period.

ROOF STRUCTURES

Many different designs are used for the beams that support roofs. Their aims, however, are the same: to hold up the roof covering, keep the structure rigid, and minimize the tendency for the roof structure to push the walls of the building apart.

TRUSSED RAFTER
This type could be used over wider spans. It was sometimes boarded over.

ARCH BRACE
The tie beam was replaced with curved beams in a Gothic arch.

TIE BEAM
This extremely simple construction was used over narrow spans.

HAMMER BEAM
This combines the two previous designs with added hammer beams.

ORNAMENTS

Almost every country and period has its characteristic ornament, and only a small selection can be shown here. Such ornament can appear anywhere on a building – around doorways and windows, in decorative cornices along the tops of walls, and in plasterwork on ceilings. It is often a good clue to the age of the building.

BYZANTINE
Architects of the Byzantine Empire often used a deeply carved "openwork" design.

GREEK CARVED FRET
The ancient Greeks used many variations on this fret design or key pattern.

ROMANESQUE
Buildings in this style are often ornamented. The most common was a simple carved zigzag.

GOTHIC FOLIAGE
Many cathedrals and churches of the 13th century are adorned with foliage.

ACANTHUS
Both the Greeks and Romans used this leaf ornament on their buildings.

BALLFLOWERS
This motif belongs to the later Gothic of the 14th century. It is often found around windows.

CLASSICAL ORDERS

The ancient Greeks and Romans based all their decoration on styles called orders. The Greeks had Doric, Ionic, and Corinthian; the Romans added Tuscan and Composite.

CORINTHIAN
The capitals of the Corinthian order are known for their decoration of richly carved acanthus leaves.

DORIC
This was the earliest order. The capitals are simple. The fluted columns do not have separate bases.

TUSCAN
Capitals of the Tuscan order are similar to the Doric, but the columns are plain, not fluted.

IONIC
A noticeable feature of the Ionic order is the twin spiral design of the capitals.

COMPOSITE
Composite capitals resemble Corinthian capitals, but with spiral motifs at each of the corners.

DOMES

Some of the most imposing roofs are in the form of domes. These are usually difficult to build, and the shape depends on whether the priority is to create a striking exterior or to roof a large interior.

HEMISPHERICAL DOME
This dome shape makes an imposing silhouette, but it is difficult to build.

POLYHEDRAL DOME
This solution to roofing an octagonal space was used on Florence Cathedral.

SAUCER DOME
The architects of 6th-century Byzantium built wide, shallow domes covering large interiors.

ONION DOME
The 16th-century St. Basil's cathedral in Moscow has many onion domes, a popular feature on Russian buildings.

TIMELINE

THIS TIMELINE SHOWS where and when some of the most important styles of architecture were used, and how they developed. There is much similarity in Indian and Far Eastern buildings over a wide timespan, whereas there are many radical changes of style in the West. In the 20th century, styles tend to become more international.

1000 B.C.-1 A.D.

CHINESE MILITARY

Great Wall of China

Parthenon

KEY
These colors show the geographical groupings used in the chart.

Far East, India, and Australia

Americas

Europe

Middle East and Africa

7000-1000 B.C.

ANCIENT ANATOLIAN *Turkey*

CLASSICAL GREEK

MINOAN *Crete*

EGYPTIAN OLD KINGDOM

NEO-BABYLONIAN

City gateway, Babylon

SUMERIAN *Middle East*

Ziggurat, Ur, Iraq

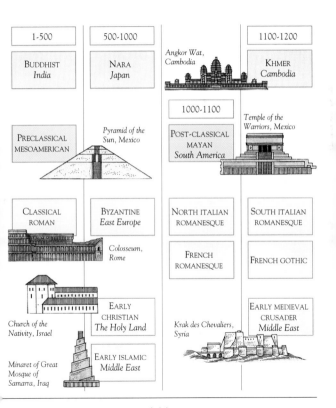

1-500

BUDDHIST
India

500-1000

NARA
Japan

*Angkor Wat,
Cambodia*

1100-1200

KHMER
Cambodia

1000-1100

PRECLASSICAL
MESOAMERICAN

*Pyramid of the
Sun, Mexico*

POST-CLASSICAL
MAYAN
South America

*Temple of the
Warriors, Mexico*

CLASSICAL
ROMAN

BYZANTINE
East Europe

NORTH ITALIAN
ROMANESQUE

SOUTH ITALIAN
ROMANESQUE

*Colosseum,
Rome*

FRENCH
ROMANESQUE

FRENCH GOTHIC

EARLY
CHRISTIAN
The Holy Land

*Church of the
Nativity, Israel*

EARLY MEDIEVAL
CRUSADER
Middle East

*Krak des Chevaliers,
Syria*

EARLY ISLAMIC
Middle East

*Minaret of Great
Mosque of
Samarra, Iraq*

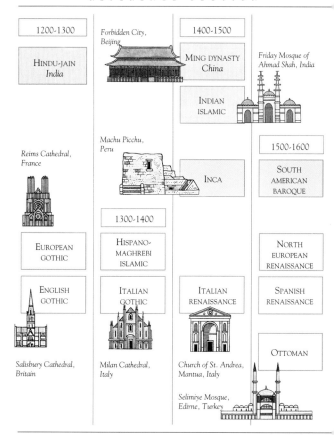

1200-1300

HINDU-JAIN
India

*Forbidden City,
Beijing*

1400-1500

MING DYNASTY
China

*Friday Mosque of
Ahmad Shah, India*

INDIAN
ISLAMIC

*Reims Cathedral,
France*

*Machu Picchu,
Peru*

1500-1600

INCA

SOUTH
AMERICAN
BAROQUE

1300-1400

EUROPEAN
GOTHIC

HISPANO-
MAGHREBI
ISLAMIC

NORTH
EUROPEAN
RENAISSANCE

ENGLISH
GOTHIC

ITALIAN
GOTHIC

ITALIAN
RENAISSANCE

SPANISH
RENAISSANCE

OTTOMAN

*Salisbury Cathedral,
Britain*

*Milan Cathedral,
Italy*

*Church of St. Andrea,
Mantua, Italy*

*Selimiye Mosque,
Edirne, Turkey*

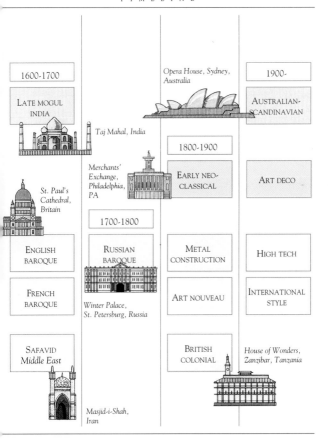

1600-1700

LATE MOGUL INDIA

Taj Mahal, India

Opera House, Sydney, Australia

1900-

AUSTRALIAN-SCANDINAVIAN

Merchants' Exchange, Philadelphia, PA

1800-1900

EARLY NEO-CLASSICAL

ART DECO

St. Paul's Cathedral, Britain

ENGLISH BAROQUE

1700-1800

RUSSIAN BAROQUE

METAL CONSTRUCTION

HIGH TECH

FRENCH BAROQUE

Winter Palace, St. Petersburg, Russia

ART NOUVEAU

INTERNATIONAL STYLE

SAFAVID *Middle East*

BRITISH COLONIAL

House of Wonders, Zanzibar, Tanzania

Masjid-i-Shah, Iran

FROM PLAN TO BUILDING

EVERY BUILDING has to be designed. The architect produces a set of plans that the builder can follow, and construction is carried out in a strict order – foundations have to be laid before walls can be built, and decoration is the final stage.

PLAN

Drawings are accompanied by notes on materials and construction.

Stairs

ELEVATION

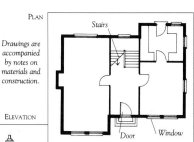

Door   Window

PLANS AND ELEVATIONS
The architect produces plans of each floor, showing its dimensions and features, such as stairs, doors, and windows. Elevations are drawings of each side of the building, showing how it will look when built.

Trenches for foundations

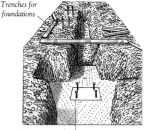

Concrete weight-bearing point   GROUNDWORKS

GROUNDWORKS
The builder's first job will be to prepare the ground, removing topsoil, making it level, marking out the position of the building, and digging trenches to take the foundations. Concrete is poured in to make the foundations, and pipes are inserted for wires, water, and gas.

SUPERSTRUCTURE

Platforms laid on
scaffolding to
support workers

Window
frame

Scaffolding

SUPERSTRUCTURE
As the walls rise, door
and window frames are
added, with lintels on
top to take the weight of
the masonry. Higher
still, joists are fitted to
take the upper floor.
Scaffolding allows
access to the roof.

SERVICES
Electrical wiring and
plumbing are fitted. Many
of the wires and pipes go
under the floorboards and
behind plasterwork, so they
must be put in first.

THE FINISHED BUILDING
After the carpenter has
fitted the internal
door frames, stairs,
and floorboards,
the plasterer
plasters the walls
and ceilings. Then
windows can be
glazed, doors fitted,
and the plumbing
and electrical work
completed, before
decorating begins.

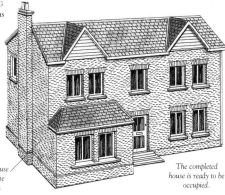

Finished house
matches the
elevation

The completed
house is ready to be
occupied.

GREAT ARCHITECTS

LARGE BUILDINGS HAVE ALWAYS required people to plan them and to supervise their construction. But it is only since the Renaissance in Europe that architects have emerged as important people whose names are permanently associated with the buildings they design.

FILIPPO BRUNELLESCHI (1377-1446)
Brunelleschi designed the dome of Florence Cathedral. He was one of the first Italian Renaissance architects.

LEON BATTISTA ALBERTI (1404-72) was an Italian writer, painter, musician, and architect. He remodeled several churches, such as Santa Maria Novella in Florence, and designed the Palazzo Rucellai in Florence. He wrote one of the first popular books on architecture.

DONATO BRAMANTE (1444-1514) was an influential Italian architect who brought an imposing, monumental quality to Renaissance buildings. He probably worked on the Ducal Palace at Urbino before designing churches such as Santa Maria Presso San Satiro in Milan.

LEONARDO DA VINCI (1452-1519) was the greatest artist and thinker of the Renaissance. Although he built little or nothing, his influence was great, especially on Bramante. He provided a model for the dome of Milan Cathedral in 1487, and a vast plan for a French city and castle.

MICHELANGELO BUONAROTTI (1475-1564)
He is most famous for his paintings on the Sistine Chapel ceiling in the Vatican, but Michelangelo was also a great architect. He added the dome to St. Peter's in Rome, and worked on the Medici chapel in Florence.

SINAN (1491-1588) was a Turkish architect responsible for more than 300 buildings. His mosques had central domes flanked by smaller side domes.

PHILIBERT DE L'ORME (1515-70)
was a French Renaissance architect
with a talent for original structures
and plans. He is famous for his
work on the
Château de
Chenonceaux,
and the Tuileries
Palace in Paris.

INIGO JONES (1573-1652)
was the first English architect to
design along classical Renaissance
lines. He traveled in Italy before
working for James I and Charles I.
His buildings in London include the
Queen's House, Greenwich; and St.
Paul's Church, Covent Garden.

FRANCOIS MANSART (1598-1666)
was one of the architects who began to
develop the baroque style in France,
sometimes combining Renaissance and
baroque details in his buildings. He
designed the Château de Berny, and
built the church of Sainte Marie de la
Visitation in Paris.

GIOVANNI LORENZO BERNINI
(1599-1680)
Bernini started work as a sculptor
before designing buildings in the
baroque style. Most of his buildings are
churches and palaces in Rome, such as
San Andrea al Quirinale, and
the Piazza in front of St. Peter's.

FRANCESCO BORROMINI (1599-1667)
was one of the first Italian baroque
architects. He trained as a stonecarver
before designing buildings such as San
Carlo alle Quattro Fontane in Rome,
which show a dramatic use of shapes
like triangles and curves. He also
designed the Palazzo Falconieri, Rome.

LOUIS LE VAU (1612-70)
worked with interior designer Charles
le Brun to create elaborate baroque
town houses. He
designed the
Château of
Vaux le
Vicomte.

CHRISTOPHER WREN (1631-1723)
is the most famous English classical
architect. After the Great Fire of
London (1666), he designed 51 new
churches and rebuilt St. Paul's
Cathedral. He is famous for his
alterations to the royal palace at
Hampton Court.

JULES HARDOUIN MANSART (1646-1707)
was the great-nephew of François
Mansart and France's first fully fledged
baroque architect. He designed various
châteaux before becoming architect to
King Louis XIV, for whom he
remodeled parts of the sumptuous
palace of Versailles.

BERNHARD FISHER VON ERLACH
(1656-1723)
An Austrian baroque architect, Von
Erlach trained in Rome and worked
mainly in Vienna. He is famous for
palaces, such as the Palace of the
Hungarian Guard, Vienna, and the
Clam Galles Palace, Prague.

NICHOLAS HAWKSMOOR (1661-1736)
was an English architect who assisted
both Sir Christopher Wren and Sir
John Vanbrugh, working on such
buildings as St. Paul's Cathedral and
Castle Howard. His baroque style,
greatly influenced by Wren, is evident
in his six London churches.

SIR JOHN VANBRUGH (1664-1726)
was a British army officer and
playwright before an architect. His
first building was the enormous,
baroque Castle Howard, designed for
a friend. Vanbrugh also designed
Blenheim Palace, and became the best
known architect of English baroque.

KARL FRIEDRICH SCHINKEL (1781-1841)
was the greatest German architect of
the neo-classical style. His buildings use
Greek and Roman
details, and
include Berlin's
Altes Museum
and New
Guard House.

A.W.N. PUGIN (1812-52)
was the English architect who was a
great advocate of the Gothic revival.
He was famous for his books
explaining the Gothic style, for his
Gothic churches, and for designing
the rich details of the interior of the
Houses of Parliament in London.

J.L.C. GARNIER (1825-98)
was a little-known French architect of
the Second Empire until he won the
competition to design the great opera
house that was to be the focal point of
Paris. After the Opéra was finished in
1875, he went on to design casinos at
Monte Carlo and Vittel.

ANTONI GAUDI (1852-1926)

was a Catalan architect
with a unique style.
His buildings feature
sculptural roofs and
mosaic decorations. His
most famous work is
Barcelona's unfinished
Sagrada Familia church.

LOUIS SULLIVAN (1856-1924)
was an influential Chicago architect
who was a great pioneer of the
skyscraper. His buildings, such as the
Carson Pirie Scott Store and the
Auditorium Building in Chicago, are
modern in that their structure can be
seen from the outside, but they are
covered in beautiful ornament.

VICTOR HORTA (1861-1947) was a Belgian architect who created the Art Nouveau style. In a group of houses and public buildings in Brussels he developed the use of elegant whiplash curves in a style known for its extravagance. This can be seen in the Van Eetvelde and Tassel houses.

FRANK LLOYD WRIGHT (1867-1959) was the best-known modern American architect. He designed a variety of structures from numerous houses to factories and public buildings.

CHARLES RENNIE MACKINTOSH (1868-1928) Mackintosh was a Scottish architect who developed an individual version of the Art Nouveau style based upon straight lines. His best known work is in Glasgow, in buildings such as the School of Art and Willow Tea Rooms.

SIR EDWIN LUTYENS (1869-1944) was a British architect who was one of the last in the early 20th century to use traditional motifs from classical design – and the old construction methods that went with them. He was famous for his country houses and for the planning of New Delhi, India.

WALTER GROPIUS (1883-1969) was a modern architect and a teacher. He was a founder of the Bauhaus school and designed the Bauhaus buildings at Dessau in Germany.

LUDWIG MIES VAN DER ROHE (1886-1969) One of the fathers of modern architecture, this German architect designed steel and glass buildings, summing up his theory that "less is more." He believed that a building should reflect its function.

LE CORBUSIER (1887-1965) was the name used by the important Swiss-French architect Charles Edouard Jeanneret. He developed many of the key features of modern building, such as the use of glass and concrete, and the idea of a whole community – homes, shops, and services – housed in one building.

KENZO TANGE (b.1913) is known as the Grand Old Man of modern Japanese architecture. His buildings include the stadia for the Tokyo Olympic Games, and the twin skyscraper towers of the City Hall at Shinjuku, Tokyo, completed in the late 1980s. He has also been an influential city planner.

Resources

Whenever you are visiting an unfamiliar town, call ahead to the local Chamber of Commerce. Such offices usually have a wide range of information and publicity material about local buildings, especially those that are open to the public. Another useful source is likely to be the local museum, where there may be both publicity material and staff who can give information about local history, buildings, and architecture.

UNITED STATES

American Institute of Architects
1735 New York
Avenue, NW
Washington, DC 20006

The Athenaeum of Philadelphia
Dept. of Architecture
219 South 6th Street
Philadelphia, PA 19106

Avery Library*
Columbia University
New York, NY 100027

Boston Public Library &Eastern Massachusetts Regional Public Library System
Copley Square
Boston, MA 02117

Carnegie Library of Pittsburgh
4400 Forbes Avenue
Pittsburgh, PA 15213

Colonial Williamsburg
P.O. Box C
Williamsburg, VA 23187

Cooper-Hewitt Museum, The Smithsonian Institution's National Museum of Design
2 East 91st Street
New York, NY 10128

Delaware Art Museum
2301 Kentmere Parkway
Wilmington, DE 19806

The Denver Art Museum
100 West 14th Avenue
Parkway
Denver, CO 80204

Duke University*
William R. Perkins
Library
Durham, NC 27706

The Free Library of Philadelphia
Art Department
Logan Square
Philadelphia, PA 19103

Library of Congress
Washington, DC 20540

Massachusetts Institute of Technology (MIT) Libraries*
Room 14S-216
Cambridge, MA 02139

The Museum of Modern Art
11 West 53rd Street
New York, NY 10019

The National Archives
Central Reference
Service Division
Washington, DC 20408

National Register of Historic Places
National Park Service
P.O. Box 37127
Washington, DC 20013

National Trust for Historic Preservation
Response Center
1785 Massachusetts Avenue, NW
Washington, DC 20036

New York Historical Society
170 Central Park West
New York, NY 10024

New York Landmarks Conservancy
141 5th Avenue
New York, NY 10010

New York Public Library: Research Libraries
US Local History & Genealogy Dept.
Fifth Avenue at 42nd Street
New York, NY 10018

Northwestern University Library*
1935 Sheridan Road
Evanston, IL 60201

Old Sturbridge Village
Sturbridge, MA 01566

Pennsylvania State University
Fred Lewis Pattee Library
University Park, PA 16802

Society of Architectural Historians
1232 Pine Street
Philadelphia, PA 19170

University of Southern California*
Edward L. Doheny
Memorial Library
University Park
Los Angeles, CA 90089

University of Texas Libraries*
Box P
Austin, TX 78713

Whitney Museum of American Art
Madison Avenue at 75th Street
New York, NY 10021

CANADA

McGill University Libraries*
3459 McTavish Street
Montreal, Quebec
H3A 1Y1

*It is advisable to call ahead to find out reader policies for college or university libraries.

Glossary

ARCH
Structure, usually curved, over an opening. An arch is designed so that it can be supported only from the sides.

ARCHITECT
Person who designs buildings and supervises their construction.

ARCHITRAVE
In classical architecture, the lowest part of the entablature. Or, the molded frame of a window or a door.

BAILEY
The courtyard, or ward, of a castle.

BAROQUE
Late Renaissance (17th- and 18th-century) style, typified by bold, highly elaborate decoration.

BARREL VAULT
Vault with a continuous, semicircular section, like a tunnel.

BASILICA
Originally a Roman public hall consisting of a large room with side aisles. Later adapted for Christian churches.

BUTTRESS
Masonry projection from a wall, often helping to support a vault or roof.

CAPITAL
The upper section of a column, often carved.

CAST-IRON
Iron shaped by pouring the molten metal into a preformed mold.

CEMENT
Mixture of clay and limestone, heated and ground to a powder.

CHOIR
The eastern area of a Christian church or cathedral, normally occupied by the choir and the clergy; also called quire or chancel.

CLASSICAL
Style of architecture used in ancient Greece and Rome, and imitated in later periods.

COLUMN
A vertical postlike support. Usually consists of three parts: a base, a shaft (usually circular or polygonal), and a capital at the top.

CONCRETE
Mixture, usually of cement, sand, gravel, and water. It can be poured into a mold where it sets hard.

CORBEL
Stone blocks, sticking out from a wall, used to support part of a building, such as a roof or floor beams.

CORINTHIAN
One of the classical orders, typified by the acanthus-leaf decoration on the capital and fluted columns.

CORNICE
In classical architecture, the upper part of the entablature. Or, the area where the wall and ceiling join, decorated with plaster moldings.

CRUCKS
Two curved beams, arranged in an inverted V-shape to form the framework of a building.

CRYPT
Basement area in a building, especially a church or cathedral.

DOME
A curved solid roof, usually circular or polygon in its plan.

DORIC
One of the classical orders, typified by plain capitals and fluted columns without bases.

DRUM
Cylindrical structure below a dome. Gives the dome extra height and allows for the inclusion of windows to light the interior.

EAVES
Lower part of a roof, where it overhangs the face of the wall.

ENTABLATURE
In classical architecture, section of wall just above the capitals of the columns, made up of the architrave, frieze, and cornice supported by a colonnade.

FACADE
The face or elevation of a building.

FAN VAULT
Style of vaulting used in England in the 16th century, in which the ribs are of equal length and form a fan shape.

FORUM
The public open space, for social, civic, or market purposes, found in every Roman town.

FOUNDATIONS
The underground section of a building, which supports the weight above ground.

GABLE
Triangular part of a wall between the sides of a pitched roof.

GARGOYLE
Grotesque or humorous carving, sticking out from a building. Often disguises a water spout.

GOTHIC
Style of architecture fashionable in western Europe in the medieval period, typified by the use of pointed arches.

GROIN VAULT
Vault with curved edges that mark the places where the intersecting surfaces meet.

HALF-TIMBERED
Type of building with a wooden frame and the spaces filled in with wattle and daub, brick, or other material.

IONIC
One of the classical orders, typified by capitals decorated with a spiral motif.

JAMB
The side of a doorway or a window.

JOIST
Beam supporting a floor.

KEYSTONE
Central stone at the top of an arch.

KING POST
Vertical roof beam joining the tie beam to the ridge above.

LANCET
Narrow, sharp pointed arch or window common in early Gothic buildings.

LINENFOLD
A type of ornament, imitating folded linen, carved on timber panels.

LINTEL
Horizontal beam, made of wood or stone, spanning the top of a window or doorway.

LOUVER
Slat that can be angled to admit air, while preventing rain or direct sunlight from entering the building.

MACHIOLATION
In a castle, a projecting parapet with openings in the floor, through which missiles were dropped.

MANSARD ROOF
Roof with a steep lower slope and a more gently sloping upper section, named after the French architect Mansart.

MASONRY
Usually, building work in stone; sometimes the term includes work in brick or concrete.

MIHRAB
A prayer-niche in mosques oriented toward Mecca. It first appeared in the early 8th century.

MINARET
Slim tower forming part of a mosque, from which an official called a muezzin calls the faithful to prayer.

MORTAR
Material made usually from cement, sand, and lime. It is used as a bond between bricks or stone.

MOSAIC
Decorative design made up of small squares of colored stone or glass.

MOTTE
The earth mound of an early medieval castle.

MOLDINGS
Decorative profile given to a projecting part, such as a ceiling cornice.

NAVE
The western arm of a Christian church.

NICHE
Recess in a wall, often specially designed to accommodate a statue.

ORDERS
The styles of classical architecture, defined by the designs of their columns and entablatures. The three Greek orders were the Doric, Ionic, and Corinthian. The Romans added Tuscan and Composite.

PARAPET
The part of a wall above the gutter, which is sometimes decorated with battlements or other designs.

PEDIMENT
In classical architecture, a triangular section of wall above the entablature. Can also be semicircular in shape.

PENDENTIVE
Curved triangular surface formed to support a circular dome over a square structure.

PIER
Solid masonry support for an arch or bridge.

PILE
Shaft of wood or concrete which is driven into the ground as part of the foundations of the building.

PILOTIS
Posts or "stilts" raising a building off the ground.

PLINTH
The projecting base of a building. Or, the lowest part of a column base.

PORTICO
Entrance porch supported by a row of decorative columns.

PREFABRICATION
Making of parts of a building in advance, so that they can later be assembled on site.

QUADRANGLE
Four-sided enclosure or courtyard surrounded by buildings on all sides.

QUOINS
Corner stones, usually the largest in a wall.

REINFORCED CONCRETE
Concrete strengthened by means of steel rods.

RENAISSANCE
The period during which the classical style of architecture was reintroduced in Europe; the 15th and 16th centuries in most places.

RIBBED VAULT
Vault in which the intersections of the surfaces are marked by projecting bands of stone that form arches.

ROMANESQUE
Style of architecture, based on the Roman style. It was popular in Europe between the 9th and 12th centuries.

RUSTICATION
A method of forming stonework with roughened surfaces and recessed joints, principally employed in Renaissance buildings. It gives a rich, bold texture to an exterior wall.

ROSE WINDOW
Circular window with patterned tracery arranged like the spokes of a wheel, often used in Gothic cathedrals.

SCREEN
A partition or enclosure of iron, stone, or wood, often carved.

SHAFT
The section of a column between the base and the capital.

SKYSCRAPER
Very tall building, usually with a steel framework.

SPIRE
Tall, tapering structure on top of a tower, usually found on Gothic-style churches.

STUCCO
Fine plaster used for decoration in low relief.

STUPA
Buddhist sacred building, usually in the form of an earth mound clad with brick or stone.

TEMPIETTO
Compact circular or templelike structures erected in the grounds of country houses.

TIE BEAM
Horizontal beam forming part of the structure of a roof. It connects two walls, preventing them from moving apart.

TRACERY
The ornamental work in the upper part of a window, screen, or panel, or used decoratively in blank arches and vaults.

TRANSEPTS
Parts of a church or cathedral built at right-angles to the nave and choir, often housing small chapels.

TYMPANUM
The triangular surface bounded by the sloping and horizontal cornices of a pediment.

VAULT
Arched masonry covering over a building.

WATTLE AND DAUB
Walling material consisting of mud or dung plastered over a crisscrossing arrangement of twigs.

WROUGHT IRON
Form of iron with little carbon. It is softer than iron or steel.

ZIGGURAT
A high, stepped pyramid, which formed an important element in ancient Mesopotamian temple complexes.

Index

Acknowledgments

Dorling Kindersley would like to thank:
Clair Watson for design assistance, Hilary Bird for the index, Ted Blackham for research on p.144/5, Robert Graham for administrative assistance, and Ray Rogers and Kristin Ward for editorial assistance.

Photographers:
Max Alexander; Peter Chadwick; Andy Crawford; Geoff Dann; Mike Dunning; Philip Enticknap; David Exton; Alison Harris; John Hesiltine; Colin Keates; Dave King; Neil Lukas; E. Meacher; Stephen Oliver; Tim Ridley; Kim Sayer; Karl Shone; D. Sutherland; Michel Zabe.

Illustrators:
David Ashby; S. Biesty; Stephen Conlin; Brian Delf; William Donahue; Poalo Donati; Richard Draper; Hamish Simpson; Simone End; Trevor Hill; William Giles; Kevin Jones Associates; Kathleen McDougall; Gillie Newman; Robbie Polley; Sarah Pond; Jim Robbins; Studio Illibil; John Woodcock; Martin Woodward.

Artist Reference:
Ursula Falconer and Hugh Shaw Stewart.

Picture credits:
l = left   r = right   c = center
b = bottom   t = top   a = above
Lorna Ainger 31br; 42cl. Arcaid/Alberto Arzoz 123b;/Richard Bryant 117tr;/ David Churchill 115bl;/Niall Clutton 114b;/Richard Einzig 120cr;/Mark Fiennes 90b;/115tl;115tr;/Dennis Gilbert 120bl;/Lark Gilmer 89br;/Martin Jones 126tr;/ Ian Lambot 125br;/Lucinda Lambton 98-99;103br;104tr;/Viv Porter 116tr; 131t;/Prisma Parc Guell 116bl; / Erza Stoller-

Esto 125bl./ B & U International, Amsterdam 112br;121br. La Belle Aurore/Steve Davey and Juliet Coombe 54tr. Bournville Village Trust 130b. Bridgeman/ British Museum 28cl;/ Fitzwilliam Museum,Cambridge 29bc;/ Kuntsmuseum, Dosseldorf 84b.
British Architectural Library, R.I.B.A.,London 113b;113tl. Bruce Coleman/ Brian Henderson 80cl;/ Michael Klinec 71tr;/John Worrall 97t. Edifice/Darley 21br;102b;109bl;/Drury 118cl;118tr;119tl;/P. Lewis 101bl;103bl; 109tl;109tr. Mary Evans Picture Library 85br;/104b. Chris Fairclough 73tc. ffotograff/Charles Aithie 74bl;/Patricia Aithie 74tr;/G.Mason 80-81b;81t.
Bob Fleumer 132. Robert Harding/Nigel Francis 94-95b;/Gascoigne 72tr;/ Tim Hall 75tl;/Desmond Harney 19bl;/ G.Hellier 69c;/Jack Jackson 43tc;/Paolo Koch 26-27;35tl;/Sybil Sassoon 34br;/ Peter Scholey 36br;/110-111;/Adina Tovy 35b;40bl;106b;/ John Wilson 73 b;/Adam Woolfitt 51tr;96 b. Angelo Hornak 119br. Image Bank 78bl;/David Gould 101tr;/Harald Sund 79tr;/Paul Trummer 95t. Mansell Collection 91t. James Morris 19br;55tl;68b;123tl. Haruo Morishima 38tr;39tr. National Trust Photographic Library/John Bethell 90tr. Oxford Brookes University 25c;31br. Pictor 32tr;70cl. Quest/Robin Bath 69b. Tony Stone Worldwide 45b;51tl;/Kim Blaxland 91bl;/David Hanson 95tr. Zefa/Derek Cattani 39bl;/Rosenfeld 131b;/L. Schranner 31tl.

Every effort has been made to trace the copyright holders, and we apologize in advance for any unintentional omissions. We would be pleased to insert the appropriate acknowledgment in any subsequent edition of this publication.